Identity Management

Identity Management

A Primer

Graham Williamson
David Yip
Ilan Sharoni
Kent Spaulding

MC Press Online, LP
Lewisville, TX 75077

Identity Management: A Primer
Graham Williamson, David Yip, Ilan Sharoni, Kent Spaulding

First Printing—September 2009

MC Press offers excellent discounts on this book when ordered in quantity for bulk purchases or special sales, which may include custom covers and content particular to your business, training goals, marketing focus, and branding interest.

For information regarding permissions or special orders, please contact:
MC Press
Corporate Offices
125 N. Woodland Trail
Lewisville, TX 75077 USA

For information regarding sales and/or customer service, please contact:
MC Press
P.O. Box 4300
Big Sandy, TX 75755-4300 USA

ISBN: 978-158347-093-0

About the Authors

Graham Williamson

Mr. Graham Williamson has twenty years experience in the Information Technology industry with expertise in identity management, electronic directories, public key infrastructure, smartcard technology and enterprise architecture. Graham has completed identity management projects for the state government in Queensland, Australia, the worldwide operations of Orica and the University of Western Sydney. His areas of expertise are electronic directories, identify management, public key infrastructure and smartcard technology. Graham is the CEO of Internet Commerce Australia and he is a seasonal lecturer at Bond University, Australia, lecturing in ICT Project Management and Information Systems Management.

Graham holds an engineering degree from the University of Toronto and a Master of Business Administration degree from Bond University. He holds the Professional Engineering designation (PEng) with the Professional Engineers of Ontario, Canada and he is a Certified Management Consultant (CMC) with the Australian Institute of Management Consultants.

Dave S. Y. Yip

Dave has over 25 years experience working in the information technology industry. His work experience includes identity management engagements with Standard and Chartered Bank, Hong Kong Jockey Club, Hong Kong Police, and a number of universities including the University of Western Sydney. His work experience covers all the major suppliers of identity management suites including Sun, Oracle, IBM, and CA. Dave's focus of expertise is in identity management security, secure remote access, single sign-on, authentication and authorization, directory service technologies, PKI, smart card technology, as well as security audit and assessment.

Dave is General Manager of SkyworthTTG (Hong Kong and South East Asia), Prior SkyworthTTG. Previously Dave was the founder and president of Gamatech Ltd. a security solution IT firm and a subsidiary of Karin Technology. Before Gamatech, Dave was employed in various enterprises including Standard Chartered Bank, PCCW, Wang Computer and Olivetti. Dave holds an Honors Bachelor of Mathematics from University of Waterloo, Canada.

Ilan Sharoni

Ilan Sharoni is Director of pre sales for the security role management unit with Computer Associates in Israel. Before the acquisition by CA, Ilan held the position of sales director with Eurekify, a leading supplier of role management software. Ilan's area of expertise is IT/security access rights, and he is an expert in the field of role management, compliance and privileges auditing.

Before Eurekify, Ilan worked with BMC Software, a leading provider of enterprise management solutions, where he managed Latin America as Marketing and Sales Director. Ilan served as the Product Manager for New Dimension Software Ltd. Enterprise Scheduling Management Solution, prior to the company's acquisition by BMC Software. Ilan holds an M.Sc in Business and Information Systems, and a B.Sc in Physics and Computer Science from Tel-Aviv University.

Kent A. Spaulding

Kent Spaulding has more than 20 years in software development and engineering with leading-edge expertise in identity management, distributed computing, and object-oriented technologies on a variety of computing platforms, including PDAs, PCs, and workstations.

Kent's area of expertise is in identity management. He is the CTO of Skyworth TTG Holdings, Inc. and is the current Chair of the OASIS Provisioning Services Technical Committee. Prior to joining Skyworth TTG, Kent was the technical lead for the SPML 2.0 implementation in Sun's Identity Manager Product and the community leader of OpenSPML.org. He was also the technical lead for the Sun Java™ Systems Identity Synchronization for Windows product and designed and developed core components of the Sun ONE Registry Server product.

Kent holds a Master of Science in Electrical Engineering focusing on Software Engineering from the University of Texas at Austin and has a Bachelor of Arts in Computer Science Applications and Russian from the University of Colorado at Boulder.

Contents

Foreword

We live in an age in which the boundaries between the real and the virtual are increasingly blurred. It used to be fairly easy to know whom one was dealing with and what they represented; a handshake, a signature, a photograph in a passport, an identity badge all played a role in physical identification. In a digital world, we need electronic equivalents to know whom we are dealing with and what authority they possess. In a corporate setting, it is essential to identify and control the way the organization deals with customers, suppliers, employees, and other users who may interact with the information systems of the company. Who has accountability and responsibility? What controls need to be in place for good security?

As this book indicates, identity management is a key component of any security strategy. Effective security requires that we can identify and authenticate anything trying to gain access to any systems. Information must be kept secure and confidential both in transmission and in storage. Data integrity must be managed to eliminate any opportunity for illegal actions and alteration. Identity must be tightly linked to transactions so that it is not possible to deny or repudiate that association.

Identity management covers a broad range of issues. This text opens with a discussion of the concept of a digital persona before looking at how identity can be managed and stored. Dealing with multiple identities is an issue that does not usually arise in the physical world but is key to successful identity management in cyberspace. This book discusses the use of directories to manage identities and explores the methodologies for authentication and access control in depth. The important topic of role-based access control is also included, as are the increasingly important subjects of governance and compliance. In addition, the book provides some practical advice and guidance on possible roadmaps for implementation.

The concepts of identity and identity management should be understood by as wide an audience as possible. We are all susceptible to identity theft and misuse of information. Although the identity management field has been the subject of considerable research, this text brings the topic to a much wider audience. As the title indicates, it is a primer in which the key issues of identity management are identified and appropriate strategies and preventive measures are covered in an easy-to-understand format. The use of an extensive case study provides real-world grounding for the topic, together with questions that assist the reader in focusing on the key issues in each chapter. This text gives students and business professionals a valuable tool in understanding the complexity of identity in a virtual world.

Gavin Finnie
Professor of Information Systems, Bond University
Queensland, Australia

Introduction

Many books begin with a dramatic statement of why their subject matter is so important. This book is no different.

Consider that in February 2009 alone, the following events occurred:

- A laptop containing employee and retiree information for 2,300 people was stolen from a Texas hospital. Data included names, birth dates, and Social Security numbers.

- A travel reservations Web site used by U.S. federal agencies was hacked, redirecting sessions to a malicious Web site. The number of users affected and the amount and type of data lost are unknown.

- Hackers broke into a Federal Aviation Administration computer system, gaining access to identity details of more than 45,000 people.

- A community college in New York State sent out a mailing with the recipients' Social Security numbers posted prominently on the back cover of approximately half of the 28,000 pieces sent out.

- Police retrieved the computer of a former employee of a company in northern California that contained the names, addresses, birth dates, and Social Security numbers of 30,000 employees.

And February was nothing special. (These examples are U.S.-centric because the United States has the most stringent laws governing declaration of privacy data breaches. Similar and more dramatic breaches occur in other geographies, but the lack of sophisticated legal requirements for transparency means they usually go unreported.)

These breaches are a direct result of a failure to provide a simple, comprehensive, and planned identity management infrastructure, with the result that staff are actually encouraged to act unwisely and, in some cases, to break the law. In such an environment, protecting identity data properly is difficult.

What Is Identity Management?

Managing identities in an organization is simply organizing the collection, storage, and disbursement of data specific to people within the organization and to persons and companies external to the organization, be they customers or suppliers. It is critical for organizations to put such management in place to avoid excessive costs and potential litigation. The identity management activity becomes a central component of the company's security infrastructure, striving to provide the four main tenets of information technology security:

- *Authentication* of entities seeking to gain access to the organization's resources

- *Confidentiality* in the transmission of sensitive information

- *Data integrity* to ensure data is safely stored and appropriately disseminated

- *Non-repudiation*, whereby someone who conducts a transaction cannot subsequently claim not to have done so

The History: Where Has Identity Management Come From?

Identity management has a checkered past. History dictates that different communities will approach the subject of identity management from different perspectives.

Some nationalities are quite content to have government track their identities. In World War II, the citizens of many countries were required to "carry papers" to substantiate their citizenship. In many Asian nations, individuals must carry documents to be able to identity themselves to the authorities on demand.

In other countries, though, the tracking of individuals and the need to carry identification papers are viewed as something akin to a police state, to be avoided at all costs. In 1987, Australians soundly defeated the proposal for a national identity card to be used to manage delivery of government services. As a consequence, on the positive side, people's identity details are not stored in any single repository, and the government's ability to monitor citizens is limited. On the negative side, fraudulent claims on government services continue to flourish.

At the company level, similar situations exist. Identity data typically resides in multiple repositories, with little ability to join repositories to form a comprehensive picture of a person's identity and access rights. This situation considerably frustrates the organization's ability to meet the increasingly stringent governance constraints that both industry and government are placing on companies today.

> Some time ago, one of the authors accompanied a high-level manager from Australia on a "study tour" to Europe to learn more about the use of smartcards for identity purposes. One day, at the Microsoft Executive Briefing Centre in Reading in the United Kingdom, a Microsoft employee who had worked on the national identity card in Belgium made a presentation. At the end of the program, a U.K.-based Microsoft staff member in attendance was quite incredulous. He turned to the presenter and said, "You mean everybody in Belgium has to carry one of these cards? We would never go for that in the U.K." To which the Belgian replied, "That's why you're getting all our refugees."

With advances in the use of technology and the increased use of online service delivery by both government and commercial organizations, it is becoming more important to have the privacy discussion to determine the degree to which we want to allow electronic tracking of our identities. The less we want to accommodate such tracking, the more we must accept inefficient service delivery.

The Current Status: What's the State of the Industry?

The identity management environment is now very advanced. Most organizations are adopting a corporate directory approach, either by installing a single monolithic directory service or via a virtual directory service that provides a single point of contact for access into the multiple identity repositories in the organizations. There is increased use of automated processes to provision identity information into these repositories and an interest in workflow technology to manage the approval processes.

It is now technically possible to identify a person electronically to a very high level of authentication. Three types of authentication can typically be used to select the desired level of identification:

- *Single-factor* — Single-factor authentication usually relies on a piece of information that the identity in question would be expected to know, such as mother's maiden name or high school name. The use of passwords also falls into this category. Telephone companies and help desks commonly use this authentication method.

- *Two-factor* — In addition to "something you know," two-factor authentication expects you to have something. Banks use this authentication approach; they expect you to have your credit card as well as know your PIN.

- *Three-factor* — In addition to "something you know" and "something you have," three-factor authentication requires "something you are." Biometrics, such as facial recognition, fingerprinting, or iris scans, are typically used at this authorization level.

While identity management technology is well advanced, people's acceptance of it is not. We dislike having to remember too many passwords, and we resent the inordinate amount of time spent resetting them. We resist smartcards because we fear they give card operators unprecedented power to track our transactions. We resent fingerprinting because of its association with the prosecution of criminals. The Brisbane airport has had SmartGate, an automated immigration entry system based on facial recognition, for some time now, but people returning from overseas with electronic passports still choose to line up and wait to see an immigration officer.

The Future: What to Look Out For and What to Avoid

There is little doubt that, despite the best efforts of civil libertarians, the advance of technology is unstoppable. We all cringed at the thought of government control as we watched the movie *Brazil* or read George Orwell's *1984*, but it is now happening. Unless you are willing to obtain a credit card, you cannot book a room at many hotels. Unless you have a security token or sign up for Short Message Service (SMS) messaging, it is not possible to do electronic banking. Without a government-issued digital certificate, you cannot submit a business activity tax statement online in Australia. And the future promises an increasing level of online activity.

It is important that this transition happens, because it is more cost-effective and efficient. Employing someone to enter customer orders makes little sense if you can get the customer to do it. The self-service approach reduces errors customers generally know how to spell their own names and addresses and it reduces cost by eliminating a job function. It also improves the customer experience. It is now possible to make an airline reservation, obtain a boarding pass, check your luggage, and get on an airplane without talking to a human being. This means no waiting on the telephone and no reliance on another person to tell you what flights are available, and it gives you the ability to choose and book your flights 24x7.

What Are the Pitfalls?

Naturally, there are hazards. First, there is the sensitive data being transmitted over public infrastructure. On a recent online session, one of the authors entered a magazine subscription request only to find out that the detail entered, including credit card number, expiry date, and security code, were being emailed to the magazine, unencrypted and ready to be picked up by any sniffer programmed to intercept 16-digit numbers. It is important that we do not tolerate such flagrant abuse of our private data.

Then, there is the sheer amount of data we enter into online repositories. Recently, on entering personal detail to participate in a time-limited offer from a business information service, the same author was asked for a birth date. There was no reason for the company in question to know this information, and such a request is a breach of privacy laws. The year of birth was really all the service wanted to know, for demographic purposes. It is important to be proactive in correcting such brazen disregard of our privacy laws.

What Is the Future?

In the future, we will see an identity environment in which participants manage their own identity data held by an online identity provider of their own choosing. Users will be able to determine whom to send their identity data to and which data they wish to provide. In the preceding example, when asked for a birth date, the user would instruct the identity provider to release just the pertinent detail for the service being requested.

In such an environment, organizations must determine the level of identity data they really require. Gone are the days when companies or government could get away with collecting data just because they might need it in the future. Organizations must determine their real need and act accordingly. The level of identity data they might want ranges among several possibilities:

- *No personal data* — The service provider needs only to validate that the user is a person and should therefore have access to service (e.g., access to train timetables). In this instance, the identity provider validates only that I have an entry in the identity data store, but it releases no details.

- *Basic data* — The service provider needs only my name and address to validate my credentials for a service (e.g., applying for a local government service). In this scenario, my identity provider would release only this basic information and would safeguard data such as birth date, credit card details, or bank account numbers that might otherwise be used to steal my identity.

- *Detailed data* — The service provider requires sensitive data, such as credit card details, to provide the service (e.g., ordering a book online). In this case, the identity provider would release only those details required for the requested service and nothing more.

The future is one in which identity management environments

- Give users the ability to control the release of their identity data

- Provide a fine-grained authentication service, capable of releasing only the requisite information and no more

In summary, it is vitally important that, as individuals, we are proactive at managing our identity information. For organizations, it is even more important to request and manage this data appropriately. Any organization that abuses the collection and management of identity data for staff, business partners, or customers faces the prospect of a hefty fine and/or jail for its directors.

Chapter 1

Identity

A person's "identity" is a nebulous concept. We perceive a person's identity as an innate definition of a person that uniquely describes that person as an individual.

In reality, our understanding of a person's identity is built upon an incomplete set of attributes that we deem sufficient to differentiate one person from everyone else, but this attribute set is generally far from complete and is at an insufficient level of granularity to uniquely define a person. We normally rely on some level of human recognition that we consider sufficient.

If we meet someone in person, we typically rely on our visual recognition of the person. If we haven't seen the person in several years, we make allowances for the fact that he or she will look older. We still might be surprised if the person has aged significantly since our last meeting, but in general we are able to "identify" the person.

If we don't get to meet face-to-face but only talk to the person on the telephone, we rely on our auditory recognition of the person's voice. We expect the accent, speech patterns, and voice inflections to match our recollection of the last time we talked. Again, we must make allowances for aging, particularly if the person is young, and we must compensate for poor telecommunications services. In effect, we are content to make compromises in our determination of a person's identity.

While this human recognition cannot occur in the online world, recognizing a person's "digital persona" must similarly make compromises. We must be willing to proceed to offer our online products and services on the basis that a person's identity definition is "good enough" for the purpose to which we are going to use it. We accept a level of risk that matches the application.

> In an identity management system, a compromise occurs at two main points:
>
> - In establishing an identity record, trust is placed in the validation of the source documents that verify a person's identity.
>
> - When a person seeks access to a service, trust is placed in the authenticating mechanism (e.g., password, digital certificate).

What Are the Components of a Person's Identity?

An identity is typically defined by a combination of

- Generic attributes, such as name, address, and contact details

- One or more specific attributes that are meaningful to the organization maintaining the identity details

Generic attributes normally apply across identity domains, while specific attributes apply within an identity domain. Within an identity domain, an identity is typically unique.

For instance, a bank will store account details, a company will store payroll numbers, and a town council will store property definitions. Each of these entities represents an identity domain, and each will have one or more identity stores. The specific attributes typically will make the identity unique.

Uniqueness is an inherent requirement in an identity store. If an identity cannot be distinguished from all other identities in the store, it is of little use to systems relying on the identity store. Organizations therefore often append numbers to the end of your name when assigning you an account on their systems to distinguish you from other people in their database who have similar names. (This approach is often the most expedient one for organizations such as Hotmail, but, as you will see in Chapter 3, it is not good practice.)

The definition of some terminology is appropriate at this point. An *identity* (a person or business) refers to the unique entity defined by a number of *attributes*, such as name, age, hair color, fingerprint, and so on for a person or name, location, business number, tax number, and so on for a corporation. A person or business can have only one identity in an identity *domain*. A domain is typically the environment in which the person or business has an identity definition. Each domain might have one or multiple identity stores.

For instance, a teacher has an identity within a school. But the teacher might also be the parent of a son or daughter at the school. In some cases, the school might define two identity domains—one for teachers and one for parents—and maintain separate identities in each, but this practice reduces the effectiveness of the identity management system. For example, there might be computer system access that is permissible for a teacher but not for a parent. If the school is defined as a single identity domain, the policy that prohibits a parent from accessing a system can be enforced, but if the system cannot identify a teacher as being a parent, it cannot.

So Where Does Privacy Fit In?

The problem with privacy is that it is intensely personal; a wide range of perceptions exists regarding what is considered acceptable and what is clearly a violation of privacy. Some people have little concern about the information they will readily provide when applying for a product or service; others will rarely divulge anything more than is absolutely necessary.

Mistrust of organizations, including government agencies, that collect personal information fuels privacy concerns. Stories are legion about hospitals that inadvertently release sensitive patient information or banks that discard client records with banking details still visible.

It is not surprising, therefore, that as the use of online services has increased in recent years, so too has concern about privacy. In a number of areas, privacy advocates have arisen with the express mandate to safeguard the public's privacy. Indeed, civil libertarians often cite privacy concerns in seeking either to stop the deployment of an online service or to severely restrict how a service may collect and use personal data.

Partly in response to such concerns, the attention to privacy protection by online service providers has improved significantly over the past few years, with notable improvement in the protection of private details about their clientele. Most Internet sites now include a privacy statement advising why they are collecting identity information and what they might do with those details. It is unfortunate that so few users bother to read these statements and that even fewer refuse to partake of the service when they disagree with the potential use of their data.

In a recent Web site development project by a state government agency for a community of companies involved in shipping containers through a local port, an electronic directory of the community participants was deployed. Company names, addresses, telephone numbers, and email addresses were collected for the 2,000 members of the community. However, the privacy advocate ruled that no company record could be published until the company had expressly consented to its information being included. The department deemed this goal to be too much work, and the site went live with only 20 records in the directory and failed to attract sufficient use to justify its existence.

Privacy Rules

Although often decried as onerous by organizations that collect personal information, the rules associated with protection of privacy are really quite simple and understandable. Most geographies have regulations in place that are binding on government bodies and legislation that is mandatory for corporations.

Privacy regulation varies from country to country, but there are generally 10 principles to be adhered to in the collection and use of private data:

1. *Collection of data*—Only data that is required for the provision of the requested product or service should be collected by an organization. It is not permissible to collect data that "might be" useful at some point in the future.

2. *Use and disclosure of data*—An organization may use personal data only for the express purpose for which the data has been collected; no other use is permitted. It is not permissible to share the data with any other person or organization without the permission of the person who provided the information.

3. *Security of collected data*—All collected data must be adequately protected to ensure no other person or entity can access it. Safeguards must be in place to protect the collected data from inadvertent release.

4. *Maintaining quality of data*—Mechanisms must be put in place to maintain the quality of the data and to refresh it periodically. A typical time frame for personal information is three years. After this time, the data is of little use and, if not refreshed, must be destroyed.

5. *Access to and transparency of data*—The person whose identity data is being stored must be given the opportunity to view the collected data and correct it if need be. A mechanism to allow this access must be instituted.

6. *Use of identifiers*—An organization must not use another entity's identifier. Bank account numbers can be used only by the bank that issued them, a medical insurance patient number can be used only by the insurance scheme, and a driver's license number can be used only by the driver licensing board within the jurisdiction in which the license is issued.

7. *Aggregation*—Unless specifically required, personal information about individuals is to be aggregated to form collective data in which each individual's identity is not discernible. For instance, if birth date is requested for demographic analysis, only counts of persons within the various ranges can be maintained; the individual data records must be destroyed.

8. *Anonymity*—Consumers of online products or services must be given the option of maintaining anonymity unless it is expressly required that they identify themselves. (Online service providers widely abuse this principle, maintaining that they need to know the identification of users. The large number of entries for "Mickey Mouse" in service provider databases belies this contention.)

9. *Sharing of data*—The collector of private data is expressly forbidden from sharing that data with another person or entity.

10. *Sensitive data consent*—Collection of sensitive data must be accompanied by the express consent of the subject to the collection of the data.

Is This Where a "Trusted Third Party" Fits In?

One way in which an organization can protect itself from running afoul of privacy regulation is to engage the services of a trusted third party. Although this motivation is by no means the main reason to use these services, use of a trusted third party does free a company from the restrictions on collection and storage of personal data; this burden is transferred to the third party.

The main reason for using a trusted third party is to avoid the cost of collecting and verifying personal data. If a trusted organization has already validated the identities of a company's customer base, the company can "piggy-back" on that activity and avoid the cost of performing the same checks and having to maintain each person's identity record.

Using a trusted third party also lets a company answer the question "How are we going to trust that the generic attributes provided by a person are true?" Although organizations have complete control over their specific identifiers (e.g., bank account number, payroll identifier, registered plan number), they have no control over the generic attributes (e.g., name, address). Other than viewing a birth certificate to verify a person's name or looking at a property title to verify an address, a company has no way of knowing whether the data a customer provides is accurate. Trusted third parties do this work as part of their service and attest to the data's accuracy.

An inherent component of the definition of an identity is the need to anchor each identity in a *trusted identifier*. While most organizations that establish and maintain identity records don't want to go to the trouble of verifying source documents, they are keen to piggy-back on the processes of those that have. Driver's licenses are often used to validate a person's identity specifically because the government department that regulates motor transport sights a birth or marriage certificate before issuing a driver's license.

However, even though an organization might rely on a piece of validated data when establishing its identity record, storing such an identifier in its data repository may well be a breach of privacy legislation. For instance, a DVD rental company might well ask to see your driver's license to validate your name and address before renting you a DVD. But if it uses your license number as its record identifier, it is likely to have broken the law in many countries. Identifiers are typically owned by the organizations that generate them.

As discussed above, relying on the identification process of another organization is seminal to the management of digital identities. In the digital world, it is easy to share identity information and rely on someone else who has done the hard work. An industry has arisen around this concept.

Companies such as Thawte and VeriSign will undertake a basic verification of a person's identity and issue a digital certificate certifying that the person's identity is accurate and current. People can apply for these certificates, and once they have satisfied the requisite "evidence of identity," they are issued a certificate. This certificate can then be provided to other organizations as "proof" of identity. Provided the other organizations "trust" the issuing authority, they will rely on the certificate as attestation to the identity.

A trusted third party follows an *evidence of identity (EoI)* process to validate an identity. A trusted third party must publish its EoI process to enable relying

While the concept of a digital certificate is quite simple, there is more to its use in the real world. Digital certificates typically adhere to the X.509 standard, which has strict rules about the detail to be included in a certificate. For instance, a certificate must include a reference as to how it can be used. In some case, it will be used for authentication (e.g., signing documents); in other cases, it will be used for encryption (e.g., ensuring that only the intended recipient can read an email message). For more information about digital certificates, see Chapter 10.

parties to determine whether the process is sufficient for their purposes. For example, a common EoI process in Australia is the 100-point check used by many banks. Under this process, a set of "breeder" documents is defined that in combination are deemed satisfactory for the verification of an identity. Each document is assigned a number of points. For instance, a driver's license might be 40 points, and a credit card bill might be 20 points. When documents totaling 100 points have been seen, the person's identity has been verified.

It is not only in the provision of digital certificates that trusted third parties have arisen. Chapter 7 discusses the topic of federated authentication, in which identity providers generate "assertions" that validate a person's right to access a service. Microsoft's Infocard provides "claims" to a user's right to access a service. These are examples in which trusted third parties are providing an important component of the identity management environment.

Where Do Roles Fit Into the Concept of an Identity?

In the physical world, identities are often synonymous with roles. We talk in terms of the bank manager, the taxi driver, even our mother as identities. In fact, these are roles, with a human being as the incumbent.

When it comes to computer systems, the distinction between identities and roles is critical. Indeed, management of roles is a major and most challenging component of any identity management system. Organizations rely on roles and often see a person's role as a defining attribute to the person's identity. For instance, a person's role will determine whether the person has the authority to undertake a specific function in a business process. A role typically defines what a person can "sign for" in approving expenditure, authorizing a leave application, or granting access to a database. It is therefore a critical component of an organization's identity management function.

A person's role is only one attribute of the person's identity and is not very useful in determining uniqueness. Multiple persons in an organization may have the same role. And roles are typically transitory by nature, with people moving into and out of different roles over time. In some cases, a person will be put into a role for a short period of time, as for vacation relief. A further complication comes from the fact that many organizations let a person hold multiple roles concurrently. This circumstance further diminishes the usefulness of the role attribute as a mechanism to uniquely define a person's identity.

However, identity management environments must accommodate the inherent difficulties in working with roles because roles are such an important element when it comes to using an organization's identity repositories for access control purposes. Given that the major reason for a company to maintain identities is to grant access to computer facilities or restricted areas, access control is the focal point for most identity management installations.

Many identity management environments are poorly planned and display poor use of roles. This situation is typically due to vendors of software with identity stores that equate access rights with roles (e.g., the accounts receivable journal becomes one role, the accounts receivable reports generator becomes another, and so on). In this bottom-up approach, a user's existing accesses are used to compute a minimal set of roles.

A better approach is to associate system access permissions with the "accounts receivable clerk" role. In this top-down approach, roles are defined by positions in the company, which defines the access rights the role incumbents should be granted.

Can I Have Multiple Identities in an Identity Management Environment?

A further complication arises when an identity management environment must accommodate multiple identities for a single person. There are various situations in which an organization might elect to do this:

- In a university, a person might be a staff member and a student at the same time.

- A help desk officer with access to the work order system may also be a Unix developer with root access to the system on which the application resides.

- An administrative clerk in the motor vehicle registry department is probably also a client with a registered vehicle.

Historically, organizations have accommodated such situations by maintaining two separate identities for the same person. Best practice, however, is to maintain only one identity and attach to that identity the various permissions (usually based on roles) for the identity. This approach reduces the administrative work required to maintain separate identities, eliminates the situation in which two entries for the same person become out of sync (i.e., a change is made for one identity and not the other), simplifies the audit function within the company, and lets the identity store maintain an accurate count of staff.

With the increasing focus on auditing and reporting of account access to computer facilities and the need to ensure that access rights are removed as soon as a staff member leaves a company's employ, a single identity with multiple roles is the mark of a well-designed identity and access management system. This design provides a level of abstraction between the identity and the access rights associated with the identity. The access rights are associated with the role, which can be assigned to an identity as required.

> In a recent review in a transport department in Australia, a check was performed between the department's human resources database (SAP) and its network access directory (Novell). Of 4,500 records, 700 could not be reconciled. Most of these were due to spelling differences between entries in the two repositories, but nearly 100 were due to duplicate identity records within the network access directory.

The concept of an identity that uniquely defines a person is inherently based on a compromise. We must determine the level to which an identity must be verified before letting users access an online service or releasing sensitive information to them. To proceed on the basis of insufficient validation of the identity may result in a service being provided in error or sensitive information being released to the wrong person. At the other extreme, to require excessive identity validation may contravene local laws and will result in excessive costs.

Discussion Questions

1. Discuss your concept of an identity. What do you consider to be the attributes that define your identity?

2. Identify three "domains" within which you as a person are identified. What are the common attributes across the three domains? Identify at least one attribute that is specific within each domain.

3. Can you think of any identity domain that uses an identifier from another domain as a defining attribute? (*Hint:* Consider your driver's license number or Social Security number.)

4. When you applied for your student ID card, what compromise did the security personnel make in determining whether to give you an ID card?

5. Can you think of a situation in which sensitive information was released after an inadequate identity check had been performed?

6. Can you think of a situation in which the security checks were too stringent—in other words, they were not commensurate with the protection required?

Case Study

This book uses a progressive case study in which we will apply each chapter's subject matter to the case situation. Although the case is provided for illustrative purposes, it is based on a real identity management exercise at an Australian university. The goals of this case are to give students an example that is as close to the "real world" as possible and to devise a solution that is progressively developed on a chapter-by-chapter basis.

The university's position is typical. It has a number of identity repositories used throughout the university that have grown up over time and are fulfilling a useful purpose. They cannot be thrown out—it's not realistic to replace large parts of the identity management infrastructure. What we must do is work from the current situation to the desired situation.

The university is distributed, with six campuses, and diverse, with three faculties each comprising multiple schools. The institution accommodates more than 35,000 students, including 5,000 international students, and 7,000 staff and faculty members.

Appendix A provides a detailed description of the case study, including the major components of the present ("As-Is") and desired ("To-Be") environments, the current constraints and issues, and the activities involved in developing an optimal identity management environment.

Questions

1. Make a list of the different types of identities that the university's identity management environment must accommodate. Indicate the subtypes you can think of. (*Hint:* What different types of students attend the university?)

2. In what areas might multiple identities (i.e., a person with more that one identity in the university) exist? Are these legitimate cases, or can they be accommodated via the assignment of roles?

3. In what areas might privacy of identity data be important? Can you think of a situation where someone might want to restrict the information that the university holds on that person?

4. Universities collect and store the date of birth for each student. For what purpose do they collect this data? In what circumstances would you invoke your right to not provide this information?

Managing Identities and Identity Stores

The main reason for a company to establish an identity management environment is to control access to company resources, be they computers, buildings, or equipment. To do this effectively, it is necessary to identify a user requesting access. If there were no resources to access, a company would have no need for an identity management environment (other than a basic payroll system). The objective of an identity management environment is therefore to facilitate providing access to resources while restricting access when and where it's not warranted.

Organizations are increasingly being required to monitor and audit access to resources. This requirement could be for security reasons, such as a separation of duties (SoD) policy that restricts the ability to initiate sensitive transactions to certain job roles. For instance, the person approving a purchase order should not be allowed to approve the payment to the supplier. Governance structures are becoming more stringent and binding on company directors, who are increasingly being held responsible for implementation of company policy regarding access to resources.

The future is an increased reliance on an organization's information technology to provide more and improved security. The identity management environment must provide both reporting and investigatory features to enhance the organization's assurance that it is meeting its duty of care to its stakeholders. Identity management environments will need to become increasingly more sophisticated to meet this demand.

Identities and User Accounts

A major challenge for organizations is to manage the identity of staff, business partners, and customers to control their access to corporate resources. Because our focus is on managing users from an IT perspective, we will consider the management of users from the perspective of mapping their identity to their user account(s). Later in the book, we will address how a user's account gives the user access rights, sometimes called entitlements or permissions, and we will explain how these rights are best associated with roles.

As you saw in Chapter 1, a person's identity is typically defined by attributes such as name, address contact details, and other identifying information. Organizations must record this information for both their employees and contractor personnel, and sometimes for suppliers and customers. This data is typically sourced from the human resource information system for staff or from the finance system for suppliers and customers.

A person's user account is typically the systems account on the company's computer system. It usually has a user name and password associated with it. The user uses this information to log in to the corporate network and application systems. Logging in to the corporate network is called *authentication*; subsequent logging in to various applications (e.g., email, portal, finance system) is called *authorization*.

Some systems also allow generic accounts. These accounts exist in various systems but are not assigned to a specific user. They typically serve system administrators or groups of users whose identities change regularly, such as classroom trainees. These days, there is a trend away from using generic accounts, and a good identity management system will require all system access to be tied to a specific identity.

Managing users is accomplished by the identity management environment. This environment consists of multiple elements of the organization's infrastructure and is the facility that stores and manages all users' identity data and access rights. The identity management environment typically provides provisioning, role management, compliance management, and workflow functionality.

The main challenges for a company are to

- Provision the access rights to new employees by adding their user IDs to the necessary systems

- Manage the access rights of "movers" (e.g., persons who change departments, persons who receive promotions)

- Remove the access rights of persons leaving the company

An acronym that is sometimes used to describe the main functions of an identity management solution is CRUD, which stands for "create, remove, update, and delete." (A "remove" is really a "disable"; an account typically is disabled to prevent access and then is deleted sometime later, after associated files have been archived.)

An increasingly important function is the monitoring of these changes and auditing of user's access rights. Most organizations are experiencing growing pressure to improve governance over corporate resources via initiatives such as the Sarbanes-Oxley Act (SOX) in the   United States, and identity management environments are being required to support increasingly stringent governance policy.

What Is an Identity Store?

An identity store is simply a directory or database that contains people's identity detail. An identity store can be paper-based, such as a printed telephone directory used to find telephone numbers, or electronic, such as the online white pages we use to look up contact details.

In an organization, two types of electronic identity stores generally exist:

- Authentication directories (e.g., Microsoft's Active Directory, Novell's eDirectory, the SunONE directory)

- Authorization databases (e.g., DB2 for MVS applications, Oracle for Oracle applications, SQL for .NET applications)

Authentication directories are characterized by short records containing just enough information to let a user log onto the network. Attributes in an authentication directory typically include user name, password, expiry, number of retries, inactive account timeout period, and so on. Authentication directories are by nature part of the mission-critical systems infrastructure of an organization. Trained systems administration staff should administer them, and strict policy should govern them.

Authorization databases are typically more volatile, with users being added and removed as their job profiles change. Attributes include account name, password, expiry, and application modules to which the user has access. Business managers, not systems staff, usually manage these lists or databases, and they normally are not mission-critical. If a user is unable to access an application for a period of time, it is usually more of an inconvenience than a problem affecting the business. An exception might be a production-control system for which there are serious consequences if a user is unable to log on.

Why Multiple Stores Are a Fact of Life

Most organizations find that their identity stores have grown systemically over time. The stores exist in a heterogeneous environment in which each application has been deployed on a different system, each running a different operating system and maintaining its own access control list. This situation is inefficient both in terms of having to provision into multiple identity stores and in the inevitable disparity that will arise between records in the various repositories.

For several reasons, it is unrealistic to assume that these applications can be modified to access a central identity store:

- Many of these applications are legacy applications, and it is neither cost-effective nor wise to modify them.

- Many legacy applications have proprietary access mechanisms and do not support standard directory access protocols, such as Lightweight Directory Access Protocol (LDAP).

- Because no planning has gone into determining the access control groups in the legacy applications, it is difficult to accommodate these groups in the central identity store.

Multiple stores are therefore a fact of life, and an organization's identity management environment must accommodate them.

The Options

The alternatives available to organizations seeking to integrate an environment that encompasses multiple identity stores fall on a continuum between a single monolithic directory server on one end and a fully distributed but integrated set of data repositories on the other.

Central Directory Server

Figure 2.1 depicts the central directory server solution. In this scenario, an organization establishes a corporate directory that acts as the storage

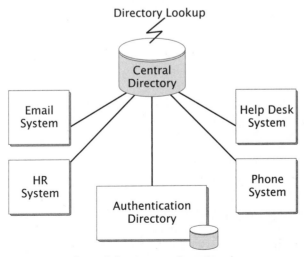

Figure 2.1: Central directory configuration

point for the main systems used by the company. Each application stores the attributes it needs in the central repository, and lookups on the identity data access this directory.

Note: Even in a centralized directory configuration, the authentication directory normally will maintain its own repository due to the specific nature of its attributes and the mission-critical status of this facility. It will, however, be synchronized to the central directory, which will be the authority for detail such as name and address.

Distributed Repositories

In the distributed repository scenario (Figure 2.2), the organization maintains separate data stores for each application, but virtual directory technology is used to link them together in real time. A lookup for an email address will be directed at the virtual directory, which will perform a lookup on the mail server to find the address, which will be returned to the user.

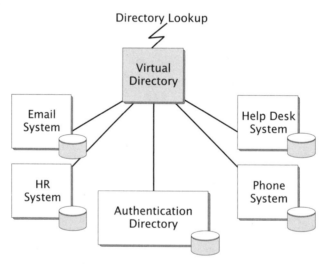

Figure 2.2: Distributed repository configuration

Virtual directory technology can perform sophisticated data joins in real time, giving subsecond responses. For instance, a help desk officer wanting detail on a user who logged a trouble report would access the virtual directory, which could return the name and location from the human resources (HR) system, the user's phone number from the phone system, his or her email address from the mail server, and the user account name from the authentication directory. This activity would be accomplished in real time via a single query on the virtual directory.

In reality, neither of these options is practical. Organizations typically have many applications that are built on legacy technology, and it therefore is impractical to interface to a central directory. Some organizations are unwilling to "put all their eggs in one basket" and will resist any attempt to centralize their directory infrastructure.

Similarly, the virtual directory approach has some limitations. Maintenance of individual repositories can be expensive from both a license cost and a maintenance cost perspective. Some system owners won't want their databases accessed during production time. In some cases, there is no way for a virtual directory to access a system that contains the required data in real time. However, integration of application repositories is increasingly the strategic direction for information technology installations.

Strategies for Multiple-Store Environments

There are many ways to accommodate environments in which multiple and diverse identity stores exist; but regardless of which option is selected, the following objectives should be targeted.

Only one identity per entity should be supported. Even though a person's identity data may appear in multiple data stores, the stores must always reference the same identity. In many organizations, the provisioning processes have developed over time and under different business environments. In some cases, new staff members must fill in multiple application forms during the first few days after starting work to gain access to the applications required for their job roles. There typically is no checking of name spelling or reference back to any identity documents. A user may enter a nickname and will be known by this name even though the name appears on no official identity documents. Another common problem is the potential for incorrect entry of names by a data entry clerk.

The result is that the organization ends up with more people possessing access to its systems than the organization has on its payroll. A person with the name "Robert J Brown" in the HR system becomes "rjbrown" in the network operating system and "Bob Brown" in the corporate directory. This circumstance makes it extremely difficult to remove all of Bob's access rights when he leaves the organization, so in many cases this removal does not occur.

Identity attributes should be entered only once. As identity stores are populated in a multi-store environment, the same identity data is manually entered multiple times. The person's name will be typed into each repository, the address will be entered into some, a payroll number will be required by others, and the cost center will be typed multiple times. At each point, there is potential for error, and once an error has been made, the company begins to incur expense. Other staff trying to locate the staff member whose name has been spelled incorrectly will waste time as a result of the error. Finding and correcting the error takes time, too, costing more money.

It therefore is important that whenever a new piece of data is collected, it should be entered into the appropriate data repository that is the "authoritative source" for that piece of data. For instance, the HR system should be the authoritative source for a person's name and address. Typically, this data will be confirmed by reference to a source document, such as a birth certificate, before being entered into the system. Every other repository should reference this data as it creates a record for the same person. For example, when a new staff member is being assigned a telephone number within the PABx telephone exchange system, the person's name should be sourced from the authoritative source for this piece of data. Once the phone number has been assigned, the PABx system becomes the authoritative source for the person's phone number.

For obvious reasons, neither the HR system nor the PABx system are ideal for real-time access and will not in themselves be the authoritative source.

Typically some form of corporate directory is populated from these source systems and becomes the "source of truth" for these pieces of data.

Provisioning of identity data should be automated. As noted above, during the first few days of employment a new employee is often faced with a barrage of paper forms to be filled in just to obtain access to the systems needed for his or her job. This onslaught makes little sense. Because it is well known to which systems access is required for each job, as soon as a person has been offered a job, a process should commence that automates the provisioning into the required systems. As the various components of the person's identity are established (name, address, payroll number, phone number, email address, and so on), they should be populated into the appropriate authoritative sources for other dependent systems to access.

Obviously, approvals are required as this occurs, and the workflow system needs to have the capacity to collect these approvals in the course of the provisioning activity.

Directory Provisioning

It is important that any identity management environment include a provisioning engine that populates identity information into the appropriate data stores. The provisioning tool knows about all the identity stores it provisions into and provides reconciliation features. In summary, a provisioning tool

- Assigns a user ID for the person, to be used within the identity management system

- Correlates the identities (groups of attributes) in all the stores through a grouping of access rights

- Provisions and reconciles the stores while providing a central place for managing identity information

A provisioning tool will add, change, or remove identity attributes, with the appropriate approval, in the authoritative data sources. If data is changed in an authoritative source, it is detected and copied to dependent identity stores via a synchronization tool that moves the new data out to the appropriate identity stores.

Managing Roles

An increasingly important feature of an identity management solution is the adoption of role access management. For any sizable identity management environment, the assignment of access rights to an individual's user account is necessary to build a layer of abstraction in which access rights are associated with a user's role, not with the individual user.

The main business drivers for role management are

- *Cost containment*—Managing access rights for a large number of users without the use of roles means individually assigning rights to a specific person, a time-consuming and expensive process.

- *Risk management*—The complexity of managing access rights without roles exposes the company to risks. Unless an individual's access rights are closely managed, the person can be left with system access that is no longer required. This possibility represents a risk for the organization. If, on the other hand, access rights are associated with the person's role, as soon as the person is removed from the role, the access rights cease.

- *Compliance*—Regulatory requirements may require the use of roles. For instance, the separation of duties policy might state that a disbursement of funds requires the approval of the accounts payable officer and the finance manager. The identity management system is responsible for tracking individuals in these roles and ensuring the policy is not violated.

Figure 2.3 illustrates the levels of maturity in the management of access rights.

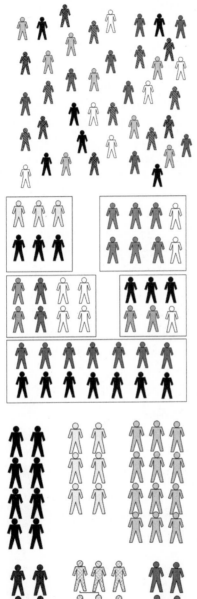

The assignment of access rights without role-based management. The system is unordered and chaotic.

Non–role-based management of access rights with each system managed in isolation. The identity management is performed in each application, with no overall management by roles.

Enterprise role-based management in which each role represents a business role of common users who have common access rights to different systems.

Figure 2.3: Access rights management levels

Role Modeling

At the heart of any role-based identity management environment is a robust role model. As you will see in Chapter 6, there are many considerations in the development of a role model, but the major concerns when starting a role modeling project are the following:

- *What is the condition of the access control data?*—In many organizations, the definition of roles varies from application to application and correlates little to positions within the company.

- *What is the first step in defining roles?*—Multiple activities typically must be conducted together when undertaking a role-modeling exercise. Not only will coordination of roles between applications be necessary, but data cleansing of accounts also will be required, until each role can be assigned to at least one known identity.

- *What role creation methods can be used?*—Roles can be correlated with the applications used within the organization, but they are best defined by starting with the positions within the company. If the business processes within the company are not well understood, the definition of roles will be made more difficult.

- *What time frame should be associated with a role modeling exercise?*— The definitions of role modeling exercise will typically transcend other activities; it will not be a one-time task that is completed and never changes. It is likely that the organization will bring applications into alignment with the role model over a period of years.

- *How does the role model stay up-to-date?*—The role model is seminal to the control of user access to company resources. It must become an integral component of management of identities within the organization and be maintained appropriately.

Delegated Administration and Self-Service

Two important aspects of identity management are enabled via a robust role model: delegated administration of the identity management solution and user self-service.

Most organizations are by nature very distributed. Companies typically have multiple locations across a country or across the world. Universities have multiple campuses in different locations to suit their curriculum or clientele. Government agencies are increasingly distributed, with locations in urban areas close to where their staff live. It makes little sense to have a single monolithic management of the organization's identity management environment. Role management means that once a directory administration role has been defined, it can be assigned to an individual, or to multiple individuals, on the basis of who is best-equipped to fulfill the role. Note that it is not necessary to follow a distributed directory model to achieve distributed directory administration; a central directory approach can also be administered on a distributed basis.

Self-service is also enhanced via role enablement. It is typically a Web-based portal application that enables the user to access the IT security repository, review and view user access rights, and perform self-service requests to add, remove, or change user roles. Users can request to be added or removed from a role, or a manager can make a request on behalf of an employee.

A basic Web portal will enable a user to submit requests, but a more sophisticated application can also perform a validation to ensure a request doesn't violate any business rule and can alert the user to reconsider a request before submitting it. Requests that are violating business policies will typically be queued in the portal ticketing system for approval by the requester's manager or the manager of the application, depending on the design of the workflow.

Pending requests awaiting approval can be delegated by the approver to "certified" approvers. Delegation, a basic functionality of most ticketing systems, lets a manager pass requests to another manager or staff member who has been granted permission to certify the request.

Discussion Questions

1. Name three advantages of a centralized directory environment and three advantages of a distributed identity store environment.

2. Outline the main costs associated with an environment in which most provisioning is done manually (e.g., via data entry from paper forms).

3. What is compliance in the identity management context? In what way can a robust identity management environment help organizations meet their compliance obligations?

4. Some systems allow only one role per user account. What problems does this restriction create?

Case Study

Refer to the case study in Appendix A in answering the following questions.

1. The university library maintains computer terminals that staff and students use to look for books in the library catalog. These terminals are logged into generic accounts by library staff at the beginning of each day, and they stay logged in until the library closes as the end of the day. Is this good practice? If your answer is yes, how would you protect generic accounts from being abused? If your answer is no, how would you manage the problem of multiple people needing to quickly access the library catalog over the course of a day?

2. The university maintains multiple systems that store identity data:

   - Student system

   - Staff system

   - Associates system

   - Contact database

   - Library system

   - ID card system

   - E-learning system

   - Help desk

- Oracle financials

- Web portal

- Unix systems

Outline the reasons for adopting a centralized directory environment. What difficulties would be encountered?

3. State why you would, or would not, recommend a virtual environment for the university.

Directories

A common misconception within IT circles is that a directory is simply a subset, or special case, of a database. This notion has led many organizations to entrust their corporate directory facility to bloated, inefficient, and poorly performing technology that is expensive to maintain and fails to satisfy the requirement.

A corporate directory has several requirements:

- It must be *fast*. Subsecond responses are the norm.

- It must be *dynamic*. Updates must be real-time, with event-driven replication across directory instances.

- It must be *agile*. Reconfiguring the directory to accommodate organizational changes must be quick and easy.

- It must be *secure*. Directories contain data that must be both widely available and adequately protected.

A database can come close to but cannot match a directory's capability to satisfy these requirements. As the number of entries increases, directories that are built on top of a relational database do not scale, and they cannot achieve the same level of performance as a directory without excessive hardware and expert database administration.

Table 3.1 highlights some of the differences between directories and databases.

Table 3.1: Directory and database comparison		
	Directory	**Database**
Records	Many short attributes	Fewer, longer, and more complex attributes
Access	Many fast reads, few writes	More updates; fewer, more complex reads
Performance	Fast, subsecond response	Less speed, more complex searches
Application	Lookup of small data sets that fit selected criteria	Transaction processes with commit and rollback facilities
Extensibility	Easy extension to accommodate organizational change	Typically more difficult to reconfigure to accommodate change
Security	Attribute-level security with read/write/encrypt constraints	Typically employs record-level constraints on read/write
Management	Focus on software configuration and schema design	Focus on data distribution on hardware and performance optimization

Schemas and Namespace Planning

The core of a directory service is its schema. The *schema* defines the data that can be stored in the directory and the arrangement of that data. For instance, a directory might contain name, address, telephone number, department, and building location. The schema defines the attributes that will store this data.

The schema is the attribute list and the rules set that determines how applications can put information into, and retrieve information from, the directory. Each attribute has a name, a description, and access controls. Table 3.2 shows an example of a simple schema.

Table 3.2: Directory and database comparison		
Attribute name	**Description**	**Constraints**
accountNumber	Customer account number	Must be unique
firstname	User's given name	Alphabetic
lastname	User's surname	Alphabetic
Initial	Middle initial	Alphabetic
phone	Telephone number	Numeric
Email	Email address	Contains "@"

Attribute names may follow a standard. One such standard used for person entries is the inetOrgPerson schema defined in the Internet Taskforce RFC 2798. The advantage of using a standard schema is interoperability; other applications performing calls to your directory will immediately receive meaningful replies.

The schema also comprises a directory information tree (DIT) that determines how the data attributes will be arranged. For instance, a flat file in which names are searched alphabetically could be used. Or, the records in the directory might be organized by department or location.

A directory's *namespace* defines how the objects in the directory are related. It provides a hierarchy that determines the way in which the data is stored and retrieved. A namespace may be depicted as shown in Figure 3.1.

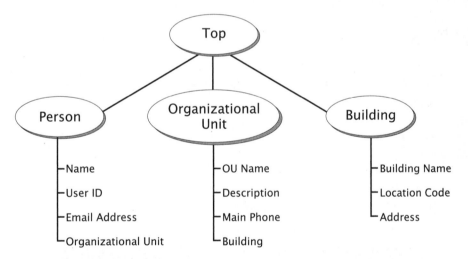

Figure 3.1: Namespace design

Object Classes

A term frequently used in the design of a directory schema is *object class*. Object classes permit attributes to be grouped in sensible ways; these groupings then define the entities to which the attributes refer. For instance, "name" in the example above is actually only one element defining a person. A person might have several mandatory attributes (e.g., first name, surname) and many allowed attributes (e.g., telephone number, email address, role). These attributes can be combined in one object class called "person."

X.500

In the early days of computing, long before the Internet and the World Wide Web, directories that stored people attributes began to proliferate. Unfortunately, no commonality existed among these directories, and they were of no use outside the entities in which they were developed. It was therefore determined that a standard should be developed that would define how data should be stored and what each attribute should be called. It was further determined that the ability to define such attributes on a global scale was advantageous. X.500 was born.

The X.500 standard defines a person's identification via a series of attributes:

Attribute	Contains
c	Country of residence
st	State/province
o	Organization
ou	Organizational unit
cn	Common name

For example, X.500 might represent the author of this chapter as

c: Australia, st: Queensland, o: Bond University, ou: School of Information, cn: Graham Williamson

This definition is fine if there is only one person by the same name within the organizational unit, but if there is more than one, either another organizational unit needs to be established or a differentiator must be added to the common name. As soon as differentiators are needed, the usefulness of the directory breaks down. If the organization includes multiple people named John Smith, adding a suffix to differentiate them makes locating their records problematic. If I have to know that the John I want is "John

Smith001," the usefulness of the directory is diminished. It is better to establish another "ou" that provides uniqueness. This brings us to the subject of relative distinguished names (RDNs), or DNs for short.

When Is a DN an RDN?

The concept of a distinguished name is central to the operation of a directory. We need some way to uniquely identify every record in the directory. Early in the design of directories, this mechanism was called the "index." Many directories are still indexed on one attribute or field in the directory that must be unique as the directory is populated — a record cannot be added unless its index field is unique.

These days, directory products are more sophisticated, but the need to make each entry unique remains. Organizations typically achieve this goal using one of two methods:

- *Adding an attribute that guarantees a unique field* — For instance, a bank can add an account number to a person's record to guarantee uniqueness. With this approach, the DN must include the account number field.

- *Selecting an optimal design of the directory namespace* — Organizational units must be selected properly to ensure that uniqueness is achieved. With this approach, the RDN must be unique within an organizational unit (OU).

An RDN, then, defines a path from a starting point, known as a baseDN. A DN uniquely defines the location of an entry in the directory information table, and an RDN defines the location relative to a baseDN.

In the scenario depicted in Figure 3.2, there are two John Smiths, but because they are in different organizational units, they are distinguished and are said to have relative distinguished names. Below the starting point of the Engineering and Finance organizational units, the John Smiths have distinguished names.

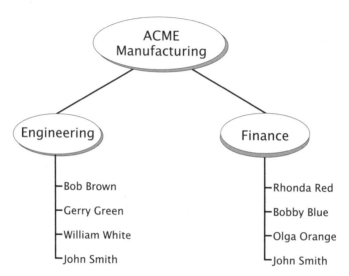

Figure 3.2: Relative distinguished names

Directory Namespace

Namespace is another directory term that is not well defined, but it is an important element of any directory design. Just as a good database administrator is worth his or her weight in gold, so too is someone capable of an optimal directory design. A well-designed directory will avoid a plethora of problems once the directory starts to be used.

A namespace defines the directory design, including the topology. How do you know whether a flat design, in which all entities are at the same level, or a hierarchical design that incorporates organizational chart or geographic (or both) divisions within the organization is required? If the directory is to be geographically distributed across multiple cities or states, it will likely be hierarchical. If the directory will be in a single instance, it may well be flat.

The namespace also defines the approach to naming attributes. As noted above, each entry in the directory must be able to be uniquely referenced. If you're defining a hierarchical namespace, the naming attributes will include the OUs being referenced. If you're using a flat design, the naming attributes may include an attribute that is guaranteed to be unique across the directory.

If the directory must support legacy systems that are incapable of addressing the selected naming attributes, establishing an OU for those applications may be the best option. For instance, if the namespace design includes a "location" OU as a naming attribute and the old Finance system cannot be changed to use this attribute, establishing an OU for the Finance system within the directory structure may be the best option. Users with access rights to the Finance application can be put in this OU and referenced in the main person OU. The directory's referential integrity will keep the user records current.

The X.500 standard provides for a wide range of potential directory designs, and designing a directory namespace is as much an art as a science. Directories that use a hierarchical model are prone to "over-design" (i.e., selecting too many OUs). (Marsupials and monotremes are both mammals — do we need any further categorization?) Fortunately, directory tools such as Groups and Referrals can help "ease the pain."

Figure 3.3 depicts a typical scenario in which a government department has several organizational units equating to divisions within the department. Each unit will contain several object classes, depending on the data to be stored. In the example, the divisional OU (e.g., Services Group) contains an object class for the OU itself; the address and main telephone number of the division are part of this object class. The divisional OU also includes an OU for roles within the division that contain the details of the role occupant.

The complexity of establishing an optimal namespace design, coupled with the difficulty of working with X.500's Directory Access Protocol (DAP), resulted in the establishment of a new standard. The Lightweight Directory Access Protocol (LDAP) was born.

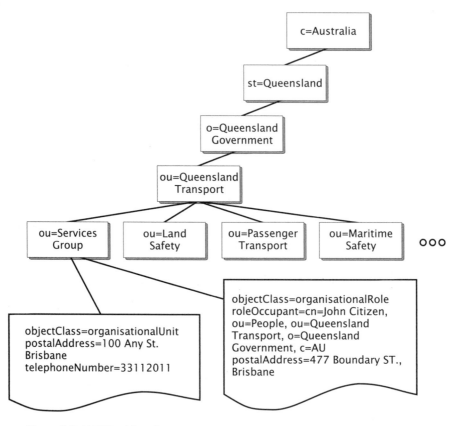

Figure 3.3: X.500 addressing

LDAP

It's important to realize that LDAP is simply an access protocol. While DAP is the access protocol for X.500 directories, you can use LDAP in front of any directory or database; LDAP simply defines how entities in a directory can be accessed. LDAP has also adopted the inetOrgPerson standard schema described earlier in this chapter.

The design of a namespace is an important part of designing a directory service. It is necessary to put some thought into it and to consider future uses of the directory to accommodate as many future requirements as possible without the need for a directory redesign, which can be costly.

The namespace design will take into consideration the main uses of the directory. Consider the example depicted in Figure 3.4.

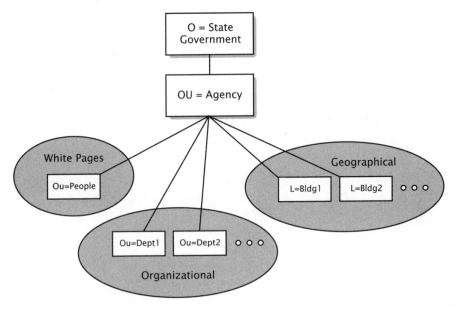

Figure 3.4: Directory views

In this design, there are three views of the organization:

- White pages — A contact lookup service

- Geographical — Details about the locations within the state government

- Organizational — Details about the departments within the agency

An entry in a person's People directory information tree will include an "ou" attribute for that person's department and an "l" (lowercase letter L) attribute for the location. Information about the department and the location typically will be held in the Organizational tree and the Geographical tree, respectively.

The Power of a DIT ⌣ *Directory Information Tree*

It should now be clear that schemas and object classes provide a structure for the grouping of attributes. A person's name is made up of several parts: a first name, middle initial, and surname. A person might also have a common name that might be a concatenation of these attributes or could be something completely different, such as a nickname. To group these components, a directory namespace provides a hierarchy: "name" is said to have several subtypes, which in turn derive characteristics from "name" as the supertype. This hierarchy gives a directory one of its most significant facilities in that subtypes can inherit characteristics of their supertypes.

For instance, a business unit may move from one department to another. The access control rights of the persons in the business unit may have inherited access rights based on their position in the DIT. In this instance, the move of the business unit will immediately grant them the access rights associated with the new department and remove those associated with the old department. It is therefore possible to very quickly reconfigure a directory to support, for instance, an organizational change. A directory can save manual intervention that would otherwise be required to laboriously perform an organizational move.

Issues to Be Aware Of

As with most things in life, when you design and deploy directories, it is important to keep in mind the main objective. Users of directories want to find information — typically details of people they want to contact. This means that the directory design must facilitate retrieval of the type of information the users want to retrieve.

However, it is often the case that users don't really know what they want, so the directory design must be able to accommodate this. Maybe users don't know the spelling of a person's name; the directory must understand this and provide the capability for a fuzzy or soundex search. In some cases, users might not want a response to a "hit" on the directory; perhaps they want to browse all people with a certain name. Sometimes they know only the first name, so they want to search all people with that name to find the right one. Sometimes they may want to browse by location, by role, or by the "manager is" attribute.

Authoritative Sources

The definition of *authoritative sources* for a directory is essential; the directory must know where to get each attribute within the DIT. The directory, in turn, is said to be the *source of truth* for applications that access it for attribute details.

Authoritative sources are typically applications that collect information. For example, in most organizations the human resources system is the authoritative source for the "name" object. This is because when a person joins the organization, HR typically performs checks to validate the person's identity and ensure his or her name is spelled correctly. The HR system should therefore be the authoritative source for the name object within the directory. The organization's white pages application needs access to this information but will retrieve it from a directory, not from the HR information system. In this way, the directory is the source of truth for name details in the organization.

Authoritative sources for data within the directory are typically found across the organization. While the HR system is the source of name, address, and position, the PABx operator typically assigns telephone numbers, the email system designates

A government department commenced a project to deploy an LDAP application that would query the department's LDAP directory and give users fast access to contact details. Rather than logging in to their email client to use the Name and Address book, users would be able to access the directory directly from their desktops.

Although the use of a simple directory lookup function held the promise of faster access to contact information, the application that was initially released failed to attract significant use because it returned only phone numbers, provided no role or organizational hierarchy information, and furnished only a search function that required exact spelling of contact names.

The terms "authoritative source" and "source of truth" are often used in confusing ways. Here, *authoritative source* is defined as the location from which the directory will populate its attributes. The directory then becomes the source of truth for these attributes to other applications within the organization.

email addresses, and the IT provisioning system establishes network access passwords. The directory must synchronize with these data stores to collect data attributes on an "as appropriate" basis. In addition, the directory must assist these data repositories in ensuring correct collection of data. For instance, the connection to the HR system might be in real time (i.e., as soon as a new employee starts with the organization, he or she appears in the directory — with a correctly spelled name). The interface to the email system might be on a batch basis in the evening because updates need to be made only once a day.

The use of a directory as the source of truth within the organization is important. The IT department must not provide network access to anyone who is not in the directory (i.e., not in the HR system). More important, when a person leaves the organization, the HR system typically is updated expeditiously because it drives the payroll system; the directory can then be the source of *de-provisioning*, ensuring network access is removed in a timely fashion.

Another option that maybe useful during the directory planning stage is to use the term "sink" or "source" for each attribute in the directory. For attributes such as name that are stored in the directory, the directory becomes a sink — that is, it acquires this data from one data store and makes it available to other applications within the organization. The directory is also the source of some information. For example, it might hold a user's account name for multiple applications used in the organization; in this case, it is the source of this information.

Directory and Database Design

Much has been written in recent years about the pros and cons of a central directory service. Many considerations apply.

On the pro side, central directories are generally easier to administer. The directory becomes the central location from which to access the directory data, and a single administration facility can typically look after it.

On the con side, a central directory contributes to overhead — by definition, the directory is exposing data that is available elsewhere in the organization. That requires interfaces to be put in place and a systems operation function to be established to keep the service operational. It is therefore not surprising that, as technology has become faster and more reliable, virtual directories have become more popular.

Virtual Directory

If it were a perfect world, there would be no wars, no hunger, everyone would live in harmony, and there would be no virtual directories.

Unfortunately, most IT environments have grown up over time in the bad old days when applications were isolationist and maintained their own identity data. This means that we rarely deal with a greenfield environment, and legacy systems are a fact of life. We cannot redesign them, we will rarely be able to replace them, and so we must live with them. The net result is that we must live with multiple identity data repositories across the enterprise running on different technology platforms. The virtual directory becomes a very interesting piece of technology indeed.

Virtual directories provide access to data from multiple sources, including directories and databases, and present that data in a single view. Rather than move data into a new database or directory, the virtual directory presents data as links; it maintains no data in and of itself. For instance, a virtual directory might provide a white pages service that presents a screen where a user can enter a person's name. The virtual directory would go to the Novell corporate directory to return the address, to the PABx telephone system to obtain the phone number, and to the Domino server to get the email address. It would retrieve this data in real time and present it as a single view to the user.

This solution avoids the replacement of data repositories but requires sophisticated technology to make it work. The virtual directory is a core component of most identity-based network infrastructure.

A virtual directory can present customer data from one database as an LDAP service to another. It can support email applications and integrate data from databases with existing directory information. Properly implemented, virtual directories can present organizational data without the performance issues of other directories. The challenge is to organize the data and map available data attributes in the different directories and databases to provide fast access to the commonly accessed data so that the virtual directory can create a unified image in real time.

Virtual directory technology can also help solve interface issues. Virtualization reduces difficulties related to LDAP object types, attribute definitions, and other schema-related issues. This means that data formats or database branding limitations are avoided. There is no requirement to migrate the data from a relational database into an LDAP directory to make the data LDAP or Web service accessible. A single LDAP call to the virtual directory service will return results from Lotus Notes applications, Oracle databases, and Resource Access Control Facility (RACF) directories.

Virtual directories can

- Respond in real time to a lookup that transcends multiple data stores

- Abstract a database lookup to a standard LDAP call

In addition, a virtual directory can build its directory information tree on the fly. If an organization view is called for, the virtual directory can perform a real-time join to back-end databases that are not indexed on organization and can create an LDAP organization view for browse or search.

But there are cons. While a virtual directory typically requires less infrastructure, its care and maintenance can be a challenge.

A State Transport department in Australia maintains a central directory infrastructure with more than 200 directory servers spread across the state. There are six regional directory trees, with portions of each tree distributed, on a master-slave basis, over multiple servers. This configuration provides good directory redundancy and good directory response times for personnel logging on to the network within their home region. But the log-in response time for personnel travelling outside their region is quite slow.

Virtual directory administrators must work with multiple database administrators and cope with changes and new releases. Virtual directories take a performance hit in that they cannot respond as quickly as a central database, but because they don't require batch updates or synchronization, they can be more efficient.

The "M" Word

You might have noticed that this chapter has failed to mention meta-directories. That's because the term has been severely abused, and there is no agreed-upon definition among the providers of directory products as to what it actually means.

In the early days, the term referred to a directory configuration similar to that provided by a virtual directory — in other words, a configuration in which the directory service does not actually store the data but knows where to locate it. But now, the term usually refers to a situation in which a separate directory is established to store subsets of data from multiple data stores. Rather than access the source database for a directory item, the "meta-directory" is accessed instead. The advantage of such a configuration is the degree of freedom it provides. If the source repository is a mission-critical piece of infrastructure supporting fast lookups for transactional purposes, it is not advisable to allow interactive access for people to browse the directory for contact details. Establishing a meta-directory with the subset of data users might require in a contact directory might be an appropriate approach.

A virtual directory would also be appropriate in such a circumstance. It, too, provides a level of abstraction between the interactive user and the production database. It also optimizes access to the source data and avoids the establishment of another repository. On the down side, a virtual directory requires another license (if the organization has a site license for the directory product being used), and the directory/database administrators need to be assured it won't cause appreciable load during production time. (Meta-directories are typically synchronized or replicated after hours during non-production windows.)

Selecting a Configuration

It might seem that the decision as to which directory configuration is best is fraught with difficulty. Although in some circumstances choosing can be complex, in many cases the decision is quite simple.

A central directory infrastructure is generally indicated if you have more than half a dozen data repositories to integrate into the identity management environment. Keep in mind that the administrative work associated with maintaining a virtual directory more than doubles with each added repository. If the organization is widely distributed, or if there are stringent response-time requirements, a central infrastructure may also be warranted.

A word about widely distributed systems: One feature of a directory is its ability to replicate itself. This means that the whole directory, or just portions of it, can be automatically copied from one location to another. Replication is typically one-way (i.e., master-slave). If the master location is modified, the change is replicated to the slave location, usually on an event-driven basis but sometimes on a periodic update basis. Two-way replication can be supported, but the logic is more complex. In these instances, the replication logic can typically override a change and reverse the change if it does not meet prescribed guidelines. This "multi-master" replication can be very useful. Once it is established, it can relieve directory administrators from mundane data versioning contention.

Note that replication is very different from synchronization. *Replication* is an internal directory function. The administrator just has to determine where to put the replicate instances, and the directory looks after everything else (provided it can obtain access through any firewalls for the ports and protocols it uses for replication). *Synchronization*, on the other hand, is a facility in which the directory administrator must be intricately involved. Synchronization is the movement of data from one repository to another. It requires the synchronization engine to support the protocols required to access both the source and destination directories or databases. The synchronization jobs are typically actioned on a periodic batch basis, but the more sophisticated products do support a "trigger" on event. In other words, the source database can cause a synchronization to occur. Most products support "delta updates," in which only the changed data, not the whole database or directory, is synchronized.

Another way in which replication differs from synchronization is that, as an internal process, replication can handle sensitive data such as passwords that typically are stored in an encrypted state, not as cleartext, in the directory. A one-way algorithm is normally used as the password is stored in the directory, and the synchronization tool, usually running outside the directories, doesn't generally have access to the passwords in cleartext, making passwords difficult to synchronize in many cases.

Central Directory Configurations

It is important to realize that a central directory does not mean a single-instance, monolithic structure, housed in the company's data center at the head office, that is difficult to update or change. By definition, directory data is volatile, and directory administration must be agile. Although a directory might be centralized, at the physical level it might be very distributed.

Logical

At the logical level, a centralized directory defines an organization-wide structure for the storage of identity data. It establishes a directory information tree that is appropriate for all the applications that use the directory as the source of truth.

In many cases, a separate branch is established for each application. For instance, if a transaction processing application requires the directory to differentiate between account types, then rather than keep the account access rights in the main person tree, we might establish a separate branch for that application. Figure 3.5 depicts an example of such a topology. The directory's referential integrity will ensure that the application's access rights tables are properly maintained.

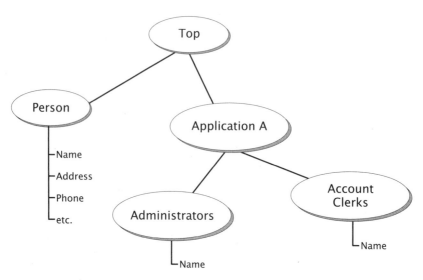

Figure 3.5: Logical topology

In some cases, such as in the Active Directory sphere, these application sub-trees are called *groups*. A group is simply a collection of entries that enjoy some common attributes (i.e., access rights to a particular application). If there are multiple levels of access to an application, these levels typically are split into separate groups.

Physical

A centralized directory is typically quite distributed at a physical level. There are two main drivers for this fact:

- Best practice generally requires directory administration to be distributed.

- Network latency and security considerations dictate local access requirements in distributed facilities.

Let's take the example of a university. In many cases, universities consist of several campuses, with various schools or faculties located at each campus. Because each faculty or school should ideally maintain its own directory entries, administration of the directory must be distributed.

Because connections between campuses typically transverse wide area network links, which are significantly slower than local area network links, a mechanism to ensure adequate response times is required. Fortunately, directories are ideally designed for operation in a distributed environment. It is usually quite simple to split directory information trees across servers and have the directory's replication facility automatically keep various instances of the directory up-to-date.

Discussion Questions

1. Name three advantages of using a directory instead of a database for storing identity data.

2. Describe a scenario in which a database is the best solution as an identity data repository.

3. State three benefits associated with virtual directory technology.

4. If you were the manager of an organization's IT infrastructure and one of the business units wanted to buy a computer application to operate on the infrastructure supported by your staff, what would you advise the business unit in regard to directory service support?

Case Study

Refer to the case study in Appendix A in answering the following questions.

The university comprises more than 35,000 students and 7,000 staff and faculty members spread over six campuses. There are three main campuses with representation from all faculties and three specialist campuses focusing on one faculty each.

1. Design a directory information tree (DIT) for the university. Would staff be in a separate branch from students? Would academic staff be in the same directory branch as administrative staff?

2. Research the eduPerson extension for inetOrgPerson. Would you include these attributes if you were designing the university's directory service? What would be the advantage of doing so?

3. Design a directory configuration for the Contact database, Library system, ID Card system, Help Desk system, and Active Directory authentication service. How would you integrate these entities? How would you provide access to a staff member's library user ID and identity card number, system details for the help desk, and the person's network user ID?

4. Would a virtual directory or meta-directory configuration be more appropriate for the university? State your decision criteria.

Chapter 4

Authentication and Access Control

Three-quarters of all businesses in North America are connected to the Internet. In Australia/Oceana, this figure falls to 60 percent, and in Europe (East and West combined) it is 50 percent (source: *http://www.internet-worldstats.com/stats.htm*). There is little doubt that businesses are increasingly seeing online transactions as a way to improve business efficiency.

As organizations embrace the use of electronic transactions, the "information velocity" (a term made famous by Bill Gates in his book *Business @ the Speed of Thought*) increases, and the speed at which they make decisions increases. This phenomenon, along with the overall greater access to information that the Internet affords, improves business decision-making within the firm, which in turn increases revenue and decreases costs.

The result is that more organizations transacting business on the Internet need to assure themselves that the entities with whom they are doing business are who they purport to be and can legitimately do business with them. Failure to do so might result in unauthorized ordering of goods, illegal transfer of funds, or malicious alteration of data.

The act of verifying the credentials (which could be identity, qualifications, or authorization level) of an entity (it could be a person or a business entity) is called *authentication*. The core activity of any identity management environment is to provide authentication services. Authentication, as the word implies, is the act of verifying a person's identity as the person tries to access restricted resources. This process most commonly refers to the log-on procedure that users must complete before being granted access to a company's computing resources. (The terms "account log-on" and "network log-on" are used synonymously.)

Authentication differs from *authorization*, which is the act of granting access to a specific computer application or maybe to just one or two of the application's features. This process is often referred to as *access control*, which is a somewhat broader term that encompasses physical access to buildings as well as logical access to computer systems. Either way, a user's credentials are compared with an access control list that determines the level of access the user is entitled to receive.

Authentication, then, is the act of confirming that users are who they purport to be before granting them access to corporate resources. Once a user is authenticated, authorization provides access to computer programs (applications) commensurate with the user's authenticated identity. This activity is a critical one for any organization, but it becomes particularly acute for a company with high-security requirements. All companies have security issues; for instance, they don't want external entities to gain access to their price lists, inventory levels, or strategic direction statements. Some businesses, such as pharmaceutical companies, defense-related organizations, or companies working in sensitive areas, must protect their resources to a higher degree. The higher the security requirement, the higher the cost to implement a mechanism that protects corporate resources.

Equally, it makes little sense for a company to spend a lot of money implementing elaborate firewalls and monitoring facilities if there is little reason for anyone to try to gain access to the company's facilities in the first place. Before an authentication mechanism is put in place, it is a good idea to conduct (and document) a risk assessment that identifies the degree to which resources need to be protected. Such an assessment should include the reasons for selecting the preferred authentication mechanism.

Another word requiring definition in this discussion is *validation*. Typically, the validation stage refers to the check of identity source documents as part of an enrollment process. Before gaining access to protected resources, a person must produce identity documents to validate his or her identity claims. This *evidence of identity (EoI)* check is an integral part of the validation process. Validation is undertaken once, whereas authentication occurs whenever the user logs on to the network. Figure 4.1 summarizes the points at which validation, authentication, and authorization come into play.

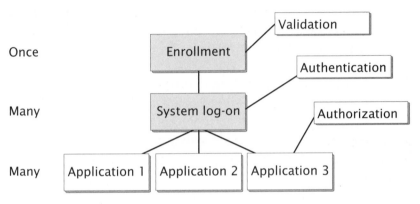

Figure 4.1: Validation, authentication, and authorization

Methods of Authentication

By far, the most common authentication method is user name and password. Approximately 95 percent of identity management systems use passwords to authenticate users, leaving but 5 percent for all the other mechanisms. This fact isn't surprising, because passwords are usually quite satisfactory for the purpose to which they are put. Remember that there are two reasons for authentication: identification and protection. For these purposes, passwords are generally sufficient.

Identification

We want to identify the user accessing our resources. When someone accesses articles over the Internet, the publisher likely wants to know who that person is so it can track who, and how many, people are downloading from its Web site. The publisher also might want to follow up with marketing material. So it needs a basic level of identification, but it has no need for a high degree of authentication. In this case, a password authentication mechanism is sufficient to enable tracking the user's interest in the publisher's articles.

If, however, a liability is associated with the service being accessed, more than just a password may be necessary. This point brings up another word requiring definition: *repudiation*. For companies that provide a service for which they must be sure the user is who he or she purports to be, passwords may not be enough. If something goes wrong with the service provision, or with payment for it, it is important for the service provider to be able to go back to the user and ensure that the user can't "repudiate," or refute the validity of, the transaction or claim it was in fact someone else who undertook the transaction. If the possibility exists that the authentication system might have been compromised, the user could in fact repudiate the transaction. (This consideration is important for transactions involving credit card payments because over the Internet such transactions are not "card-present" transactions; they are conducted under "money order, telephone order," or MOTO, rules and in most countries can be repudiated.)

Protection

We want to protect our resources from inappropriate or harmful use. If we find that a user is misusing our service, we want to be able to go back to the user to rectify the situation. For this purpose, password protection is likely satisfactory.

If a greater level of authentication is required, we have multiple options:

- *One-time password* — In this scenario, users are issued a hardware token that is synchronized with the organization's back-end systems. A display on the token shows a number that changes approximately every minute. When users log in, the system prompts them to enter the current number to substantiate that they are who they purport to be. If a token is lost, the organization must be advised immediately so that the device can be taken out of service.

- *Challenge response* — This method is widely used in password self-service applications. The Achilles heel of a user-name/password authentication mechanism is the problem of users forgetting their passwords. Most organizations can attest to the high number of help-desk calls to renew passwords. Most businesses now use a password reset facility that requires users to establish one or more challenge questions and their response. When a user wants to change his or her password, a challenge in the form of one or more questions is issued; upon receiving the correct response, the system updates the password.

- *Digital certificate* — Issuing a digital certificate to a user requires evidence of the completion of an identity step, in which the user is required to produce one or more forms of identification before the certificate is issued. Accompanying the certificate is a private key that must be safeguarded. Often, this key is provided on a token storage device, such as a smartcard or a USB memory stick.

- *Biometrics* — Another form of authentication that is generally considered more secure uses biometric identification. A high level of confidence can be provided with the storage of users' biometric detail. Popular biometrics include fingerprints, facial image templates, and iris scans. These authentication methods obviously require the installation of hardware that users can access, and they are not generally used by organizations with a controlled population. One area in which biometrics are being used with members of the public is electronic passports.

Combining Authentication Methods

By combining authentication methods, organizations can increase the security, and therefore the protection, that an authentication scheme provides.

One-factor Authentication

Single-factor authentication mechanisms typically rely on "something you know," and this something is usually a password. (Passwords fall into a category of authentication known as *shared secret* methodology. This mechanism is widely used for over-the-phone authentication and self-service password resets.) Under such a method, if you can enter your user name and password, you will be granted access to the system. This approach provides a relatively weak form of authentication because one user might give his or her password to someone else, allowing the second individual to fraudulently access the system in question.

Varying strengths are associated with passwords. Many systems require a password to be a combination of letters and numbers and to include at least one case change. Some systems require the use of at least one special character in the password.

Unfortunately, one simple mechanism to ensure a strong password is often obviated by the system itself. Permitting a user to select a phrase as the password reduces the possibility that the user will forget the password and lessens the likelihood that a brute-force attack will be successful, but many systems restrict password length to 15 characters, and some legacy systems support only eight characters.

Some single-factor, or "shared information," authentication systems use a more sophisticated challenge-response methodology that includes multiple "questions" that the user must answer correctly to be authenticated. In this situation, users establish one or more questions to which they, and only they, would be expected to know the answer. The system stores the responses, enabling persons (or systems) to verify that they are who they say they are because they know the answers. A typical question is "What is your mother's maiden name?" or "Where did you first go to high school?" or "What is your favorite color?" Systems may ask multiple questions and accept a combination of correct answers.

Two-factor Authentication

Two-factor authentication mechanisms typically rely on "something you know" and "something you have." Users are required not only to know a password (or PIN) but also to have something, such as a security dongle that plugs into the USB port or a smartcard that must be inserted into a card-reader receptacle, to gain access to the system.

One-time passwords also fall into this category because they rely on the possession of a hardware device that displays the required password. When prompted by the system being accessed, the user reads the password currently displayed on the hardware device and enters it into the system. The user can be identified because the system knows the password being displayed on each device at any point in time. Passwords typically change every minute or so to ensure that the user has the device at the exact time he or she is authenticating to the system.

Three-factor Authentication

Three-factor authentication mechanisms require users to display "something you know," "something you have," and "something you are." In this instance, a user might be required to carry a smartcard with a biometric feature on it. Typically, biometrics are fingerprints or facial templates that carry the unique characteristics of the user's fingerprint or facial features.

In a typical three-factor authentication system, a user plugs the smartcard into a reader (something you have), types in a PIN (something you know), and has a facial recognition system verify the facial template (something you are).

Choosing a Methodology That's Right for You

Although the preceding discussion indicates the normal selection of one-, two-, and three-factor authentication mechanisms, in reality you can combine these authentication methods in any way to meet the required protection:

- Something you know (shared secret)
- Something you have (dongle, token card, signed and verified certificate)
- Something you are (biometrics)

These methods can be used together in any number of ways. Each factor is something verifiable, and as they are combined, they provide stronger authentication. Even if a biometric method (considered quite strong) is selected on its own, it is still a single-factor authentication schemes.

Similarly, a two-factor authentication scheme isn't always something you know plus something you have; a two-factor scheme might combine a password with biometrics.

Also note that while more factors are generally associated with greater security, each additional authentication method represents more inconvenience for users. It is important for authentication schemes not to impose an authentication method just because they can; the scheme must match the level of authentication required to provide the desired level of protection and security.

Levels of Authentication

The levels of authentication cover a continuum from a simple password system to an elaborate public key infrastructure (PKI) installation. Companies and governments typically recognize four levels of authentication. (We exclude the additional "no authentication" level here. Organizations should not install an authentication mechanism unless it is really required.)

As Figure 4.2 depicts, as the level of risk (gauged by the severity of consequence in the event that the risk is triggered) increases, the authentication mechanism must change appropriately.

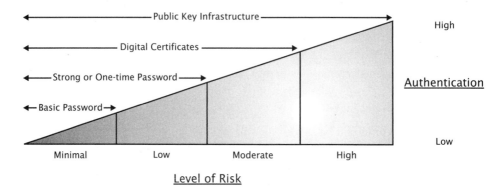

Figure 4.2: Levels of risk vs. authentication

At a basic, or minimal, risk level, a user-name/password authentication mechanism will suffice. At a somewhat higher level of risk, it might be necessary to implement a strong password format with a minimum length and the inclusion of mandatory character types. At a moderate level of risk, the organization might need to issue participants a digital certificate, kept either on their PC or on a token storage device such as a smartcard. At a high risk level, it will be necessary to implement a public key infrastructure whereby each participant is issued an asynchronous private-public key-pair with a public key certificate.

Authentication Assurance Levels

It should be obvious by now that an identity management environment cannot be designed without a good understanding of the risks associated with access to the resources being managed by the selected authentication mechanism. It is necessary, therefore, for the level of assurance provided by that mechanism to match the protection need. An assessment of the required level of assurance will determine the selection of the most appropriate authentication mechanism.

The four levels of risk identified in Figure 4.2 can be mapped onto the level of assurance as set out in Table 4.1.

Table 4.1: Risk levels and associated consequences	
Risk level	**Consequences of compromise**
Minimal	• Insignificant inconvenience to either party • No release of private or sensitive information • No threat to commercial or government interests • No opportunity for associated criminal activity
Low	• Possible inconvenience to either party • No release of private or sensitive information • Minor threat of financial loss to either party • No threat to government interests • No opportunity for associated criminal activity
Moderate	• Significant inconvenience to either party • Possible release of private or sensitive information • Threat of significant financial loss to either party • Threat to non-national security government interests • Possible opportunity for associated criminal activity
High	• Major inconvenience to either party • Release of private or sensitive information • Significant financial loss to either party • Threat to government interests • Threat to national security • Opportunity for associated criminal activity

Registration Assurance Levels

While the initial registration process of an authentication mechanism normally will match the mechanism's assurance level, it is worth noting that this process is an important part of any identity management facility. Put bluntly, a full-blown public certificate infrastructure will technically provide a bulletproof solution to most authentication requirements, but if you can drive a truck through the registration process, your solution is a total waste of effort and money.

The registration process for any authentication mechanism should match the level of assurance that the mechanism purports to provide. Again, the registration rigor should be evaluated on a four-level scale, as Table 4.2 describes.

Table 4.2: Registration process requirements	
Confidence level	**Registration process description**
Low	Self-registration provision of basic identity data (name, address, and contact details) is conducted, but no validation of documentation.
Medium	Some validation of identity details is performed with self-registration (e.g., ZIP code check, email address validation), but manual validation is typical.
High	A recognized evidence of identity check is performed with sighting of appropriate identity documents.
Very high	A substantial in-person evidence of identity check is performed, with a formal validation of identity documents and retention of proof.

It is important that the evidence of identity check performed as part of the identity validation matches the requirement of the authentication mechanism.

The 100-point check conducted by financial institutions in Australia is a popular one but should be reviewed before adoption to ensure that the correct attributes are being verified. This check classifies identity documents according to their veracity and credibility. Documents such as birth certificates and passports are typically category A documents, worth 70 points. Documents of a less robust nature, such as driver's licenses, mortgage documents, or student cards, are category B documents and are of less value typically 25, 35, or 40 points. To satisfactorily complete an

EoI check, an applicant must show one category A document and sufficient category B documents to compile the requisite 100 points.

Table 4.3 shows the risk matrix that combines the authentication assurance rating and the identity registration assurance rating.

Table 4.3: Authentication risk matrix				
Registration assurance	**Authentication assurance**			
	Minimal	Low	Moderate	High
Low	⇕			
Medium	⇕	⇕		
High			⇕	⇕
Very High				⇕

The minimal authentication assurance level will command either an unvalidated registration process or a medium registration process in which there is a basic level of validation. The low assurance level will need at least a basic level of identity validation. The moderate level will require a check of identity credentials. The high level will require a substantial check, possibly via a third-party registration authority. Remember, the high level often will require non-repudiation and be associated with a significant financial liability. For this reason, the registration agent may be required to retain copies of identity documentation.

Access Control

Authentication is the basic mechanism for restricting access to a company's corporate resources. These resources are typically computer resources but also can include physical access to the company's buildings or equipment. If someone has been issued a password, digital certificate, or other authentication mechanism, that person has been given the "keys to the kingdom." He (or she) can access whatever he has been authorized for, can request extended access rights, and will retain that access until it is rescinded.

Identity management is crucial to managing this access and protecting the corporation's assets.

Identities and Access Control

Authorization or access control is the "raison d'être" for most identity management deployment. While there may be some benefit inherent in effectively and efficiently managing the identities within an organization, these activities are usually conducted for the purpose of granting access to restricted facilities, both virtual and physical.

Access control, by definition, must be real-time. As a user attempts to gain access to a computer application, the access control system must provide the user credentials to enable the user to gain the appropriate access. For instance, an account clerk might get access to the company's financial system to allow the entry of a customer transaction. The finance manager, however, will require far greater access to be able to create reports and monitor all activity in the system. It is the access control mechanism that will provide this differentiation.

Controlling access to computer applications is becoming more important for organizations as the focus on properly managing access to documents and files increases. It is important that access be available only based on a proven identity validated by a trusted entity. This access must be integrated with the organization's identity management environment. In too many companies, the access control mechanism is independent and open to discrepancy.

Single Sign-on

One of the biggest issues with a disassociated access control mechanism is the potential for multiple sign-ons. Once a user has logged on to the company system, he or she must then individually log on to various applications, retyping user names that often differ between applications and entering passwords that are not synchronized (i.e., when one system forces a password change, it is not copied to other systems). Often, the password change frequency isn't synchronized either, with some applications requiring changes every month, some every 90 days, and some never. The result is that users are forced to remember multiple user names and passwords and often resort to unsafe practices such as keeping written records of passwords or not changing their passwords at regular intervals.

For these reasons, there is a growing emphasis on *single sign-on (SSO)*—integrating the access control mechanisms for multiple applications.

Enterprise SSO

Enterprise SSO refers to the integration of the main corporate applications. This integration is typically quite difficult to achieve because the corporate applications are often spread over multiple types of systems. For example, the main enterprise resource planning system might be on an IBM mainframe, the corporate financial system might be an Oracle application on an IBM i system, and the corporate email might be Microsoft Exchange Server 2007. Each of these applications typically will have a separate access authorization mechanism populated individually by separate administrators. This is a common but very costly environment. Not only does it require multiple administrators to keep the access control lists up-to-date, but it also means that inevitably there will be differences between the applications (e.g., some users not removed when they leave the organizations, some with their names spelled differently in different applications) and the need for users to remember multiple passwords.

To integrate this environment is not trivial. While some applications operating in a Microsoft environment can be managed with Windows Integration, non-Windows applications remain hard to integrate into a single authorization environment. Sometimes the best that can be accomplished is the synchronization of the underlying identity stores.

Web SSO

One area in which integration of applications is typically easier to achieve is the Web environment. Users may be connecting to multiple applications, but they are all operating in a common environment. Once a user has logged on, the access control credentials are more easily passed between applications. There are multiple ways to achieve this integration, depending on the ways in which each application grants access to users. As Figure 4.3 illustrates, some applications maintain their own identity repositories.

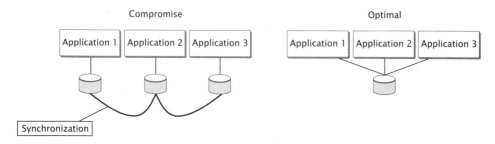

Figure 4.3: Multiple vs. single identity stores

There are two requirements for moving to the optimal solution:

- The data store must have the capability of handling the sophistication required in the dependent applications.

- The applications must be capable of communicating with the central directory.

In many cases, the applications are legacy systems that were built to operate only with their data stores, and it would be foolhardy to try to modify them. In such cases, synchronization is the preferred strategy. However, the enterprise architecture of an organization should mandate the approach for any further application development or acquisition. Increasingly, all applications are required to be LDAP-capable, and in some cases in which federated authentication is required, companies are mandating Security Assertion Markup Language (SAML) compliance.

While support for the same version of SAML between two applications does not guarantee interoperability, it does heighten the chances of achieving it. SAML will look after the sharing of messages and ensure they are intelligible to both parties; the sender and receiver must agree on the content and meaning of the message component. The Extensible Access Control Markup (XACML), discussed later in the chapter, helps.

Fine-grained Access Control (a.k.a. Entitlement Management)

With the growing focus on compliance, be it forced or self-imposed, there is an increasing call on IT infrastructure to provide *fine-grained access control*, also called entitlement management.

While access control provides protection in that users are granted access only to the resources specifically enabled by the permissions they are granted, fine-grained control goes further, restricting access to specific times of day or to specific features available in the facility. For instance, students may be granted access to a laboratory only during class time; outside of class time, the facility will not be available. To accomplish this fine-grained level of control, we need a more sophisticated authorization mechanism.

A fine-grained access control environment will typically divide the specific functions required into discrete points, as depicted in Figure 4.4. This level of abstraction provides a better design that allows for the selection of the best product for each component of the environment.

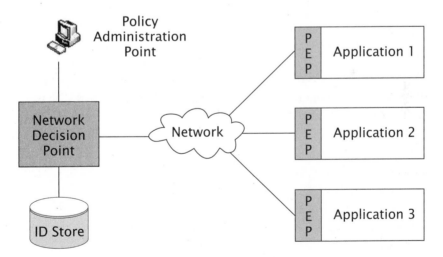

Figure 4.4: Fine-grained access control

The *policy decision point (PDP)* is the component of the environment that matches access requests with the criteria for access and notifies the *policy enforcement point (PEP)*. The PEP is the point at which access requests are granted or refused. The *policy administration point (PAP)* is the facility used to manage policy definitions.

Much effort has been expended over the past few years to define a standard for fine-grained access control and for the transmission of entitlement messages between PDP and PEPs. The result is the XACML standard, whereby entitlement decisions can be communicated between PDPs and PEPs.

XACML

The Extensible Access Control Markup language is a policy language that lets application administrators set the access control parameters for users of their applications. XACML combines both a data schema and associated language to combine complex rules and associated logic to make real-time decisions about a user's access rights to the application.

The policy enforcement point passes the policy set to the policy decision point, which passes the user information through its logic and returns the authorization decision. The PEP then responds to the user's request with the appropriate response.

A policy set consists of a target, a rule, and an obligation. The target contains the conditions that the user (subject) must meet to access the resource and the action required to meet the policy set. Successfully meeting the policy set or rule will return a "permit" decision to the PEP.

Discussion Questions

1. In what way do the attributes required for authentication differ from those required for authorization? Which are more volatile?

2. Why does authentication typically use a directory and authorization typically use a database? Discuss.

3. Both MasterCard and Visa have introduced higher-level authentication mechanisms with their MasterCard Secure and Verified by Visa programs. If the purpose of authentication is primarily to

identify and protect, who are these programs identifying and who are they protecting? Discuss.

4. Why is an integrated identity data store more difficult to attain than a distributed system with synchronization between data stores? Discuss which approach is preferable.

5. Why is Web SSO easier to achieve than enterprise SSO?

6. Think of a situation in which fine-grained access control would be beneficial. What are the attributes that a policy decision point would need to know before it could grant access to a user?

Case Study

Refer to the case study in Appendix A in answering the following questions.

1. A large part of the enrollment process is out of the university's control. It is conducted by a government university admissions office, with files of prospective students periodically passed to the university. What are the advantages of such a system to the university? Are there any disadvantages?

2. When a new staff member joins the university, that person is entered in the HR system, and, when approved by the HR manager, a nightly batch process populates the authentication directory (Active Directory). Discuss why this process is efficient or inefficient. How might you redesign the authentication process?

3. Would you consider the university systems to be high security or low security? What systems within the university might warrant digital signatures? What level of assurance do digital signatures relate to?

Chapter 5

Provisioning

The benefits associated with any identity management environment are directly related to the design and operation of the provisioning process. *Provisioning* is the population of the identity stores in an organization. In many organizations, provisioning is a fragmented procedure that involves a mix of online functions and many manual processes that are required to let users log on and gain access to the applications required to perform their jobs.

Some texts define provisioning as the act of establishing access rights to computer applications, but this definition ignores the differentiation between authentication and authorization that we addressed in Chapter 4. Although in the past provisioning processes have been restricted to one or two applications and not integrated with system authentication, a well-designed provisioning process will accommodate both authentication, or the provision of access to the network, and authorization, or the granting of access rights to computer applications. Unfortunately, a proper provisioning process that is integrated with the authentication and authorization mechanisms remains a "pipe dream" for many organizations.

The provisioning task is important, but with the increased focus on governance issues in many organizations today, a de-provisioning process is also required. *De-provisioning* effectively removes access rights for people who have left the organization's employ. Stories are legion of cases in which staff return to an employer after many years' absence only to find they still have an active account on the organization's computer network. Besides the obvious security issues, this situation likely has direct cost impact as well, with the company paying license fees for accounts no longer used.

De-provisioning normally does not delete accounts. A staff member might return, and maintaining accounts for a few weeks could save a lot of work. It is also normal for files and email to be archived before removing an account completely. The de-provisioning process simply makes the account inactive in the authentication directory and in the integrated application data stores and relies on an inactive account process, typically run once a month, to remove accounts.

A mechanism to de-provision accounts in a timely way when a staff member leaves a company is no longer a luxury; it is a necessity in today's environment, in which compliance with company policy and government regulation is a requirement. De-provisioning is actually more straightforward than provisioning because there are few decisions to be made and typically no approvals required.

The Mark of a Robust Process

The robustness of any provisioning system is directly related to two characteristics:

- The minimization of data entry

- The capture of identity data at the earliest point in the provisioning process

Ideally, any component of an identity data record should be collected and entered only once. This principle effectively means integration of the identity stores within an organization. In the past, it has been acceptable for one person to enter a new hire's name into the company's authentication repository (e.g., Active Directory, Novell, Oracle, Sun ONE) and for someone else to type the same name into the mail system (e.g., Lotus Notes, Microsoft Exchange, Novell GroupWise), but the potential for user name discrepancy and the need to unify passwords make this type of provisioning no longer sustainable.

Equally important is to collect identity data at the earliest point in the business process. This practice both reduces data entry within the organization and improves data accuracy.

Typically, the first place a person's name is entered into one of a company's computer systems is the human resources or payroll system to allow the employee to be paid. Furthermore, the HR system is usually the one place in which a person's name is validated via a check of the new hire's birth certificate or marriage certificate. It therefore makes sense to use this name record throughout the organization to ensure that the name is always spelled correctly and that no one else has to waste time typing it in.

An even better option is to not have to enter a person's name at all. The first time a name is entered into a company computer system is during the recruitment process. This means that the name and address are captured via a job search mechanism that is hopefully online. The applicant types his or her identity information into a system that collects prospective job applicant information; this data should then be converted into an employee record when the person joins the organization. All the HR department then needs to do is to sight the requisite identity documents and verify the spelling of the new hire's name.

The advantages of collecting data at the earliest point in the business process are

In one government department, the provisioning process was as follows:

1. The staff member's name and address are verified from a birth or marriage certificate and entered into the organization's SAP HR system at some time before the first pay run.
2. The staff completes a paper form to request an account on the Novell directory for network access; IT service desk personnel enter this information. No validation of the staff member's name is performed.
3. The same form is sent to the Lotus Notes administration group, who enter the name a third time to establish an email account.

It is hardly surprising that an audit identified more than 700 discrepancies in a population of 4,500 users.

- Reduced data entry

- Improved accuracy

- More efficient provisioning process with the possibility of a "zero-day start"

Zero-day Start

Obtaining a zero-day start is the "holy grail" of many identity management environments. Zero-day start refers to the situation in which the required systems provisioning occurs before a new hire's commencement of duties so that the new employee can gain access to the organization's computer facilities on the first day of work and is able to immediately begin productive work.

This ideal contrasts with what typically happens in many companies. New hires are shown to a desk with a computer on it that they cannot use to access the applications needed for their job functions and with a telephone that never rings because there is no way for anyone to find new employees' phone numbers. Each new user then spends days finding forms, filling them out, getting them signed, and submitting them for data entry. In today's business climate, companies can ill afford such inefficiencies.

Business System Issues

As with many technology-intensive business solutions, it is not the technology that poses the problem; it is the business processes. In many organizations, the IT department owns the provisioning process, particularly for network access. Provisioning is, however, a business process that is ideally owned by a business unit. The initial collection of employee data and equipping of employees with the tools to perform their job is part of the induction process, which is either an HR function or a function of the new hire's business unit.

In high-security situations in which the new hire must be granted a security badge for access to restricted areas, it is typical for the HR department to own the induction process to ensure it is conducted properly and uniformly across the organization. In most cases, however, the new hire's business unit conducts the induction process and ensures adequate access to computer facilities is provided to the new staff member. This needs to be done on a timely basis.

It doesn't matter which option, or other variant, is adopted, but it does matter if confusion exists about which model is being followed. If there is uncertainty as to who is responsible for the induction process, it is not possible to establish a robust provisioning process. Unfortunately, in many organizations the HR department considers that its job finishes with the payroll, and it fails to get adequately involved in the provisioning process. The result is that a gulf exists between the portion of the employee induction process conducted by the HR department and the identity provisioning performed by the new employee's business unit. This situation makes it impossible to conduct an efficient commencement process for new staff members.

In Figure 5.1, the organization's HR department has moved beyond managing just the payroll in the organization and has taken responsibility for managing identities. HR manages not only in the HR system but also in the provisioning mechanisms within the company.

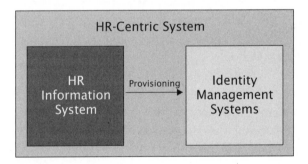

Figure 5.1: HR-centric model

In Figure 5.2, the HR department still manages the identities within the organization but only in the HR system. Identity records in dependent systems are managed via a connector from the HR system, which remains the authoritative source for much of the personnel data record.

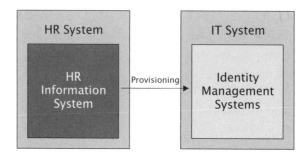

Figure 5.2: Diversified model

Either model allows the synchronization of employee data across the organization's identity stores, but if HR refuses to accommodate the provisioning process and ensure timely entry of new hires into the HR system, the business unit will be forced to duplicate data entry and generate a second repository, which will be costly to reconcile. Without a clear directive from upper management and the adoption of enterprise-wide architecture, the problem of jurisdiction will continue to frustrate the provisioning process.

Enlightened HR managers no longer restrict their activities to the boundaries of the HR system. They take responsibility for identities in the organization. This approach includes contract staff as well as employees and recognizes HR events as the trigger for all provisioning and de-provisioning within the organization.

Further along the provisioning supply chain, another business problem is often encountered. IT groups are very protective of their authentication directory. This feeling is understandable because the directory is a mission-critical piece of infrastructure that, if broken, quickly advertises IT incompetence throughout the organization.

For this reason, the keepers of the authentication directory, such as the Active Directory administrators, often hold powerful positions within the organization, with their protection of the directory becoming policy. Should an application owner in one of the business units want a change to the Active Directory schema to support his or her application, the request will often be refused, relegating the administration of the application to "lesser" staff who must manage the application's identity repository on their own. The provisioning engine must accommodate these business issues and ensure that the approval workflow accurately respects the various jurisdictions managing the identity stores across the organization.

Workflow

If provisioning is the elixir of identity management, workflow is the chalice. Without workflow, provisioning cannot occur in a robust and efficient manner. Robustness is needed to ensure the organization's policies and security safeguards are observed as the provisioning process proceeds; efficiency is needed to ensure the automated process avoids the delays and lack of governance that typically exist in a manual process.

A workflow engine must correctly observe the approval processes within the organization. For instance, the new employee's manager will typically approve the employee's addition to the authentication directory, a business manager will approve access to the appropriate file shares, and group owners will approve access to SharePoint groups. The workflow must accommodate this diversity of need. In addition, the workflow must handle leave and temporary reassignment situations. If a new hire's placement must be approved by a manager who is on vacation, the workflow process must be programmed to escalate a missing approval, or send to a "pool" of potential approvers.

The workflow engine also must be fully auditable. All actions must be logged, and an auditor should be able to quickly discern who approved a placement and verify that company policy has been observed in the granting of access rights to a new hire or a change of access rights for an existing staff member. As governance processes improve, organizations are increasingly turning to system support to troll through system logs and report on policy violations. Identity management environments must support this requirement.

The Role of Roles

While we leave a more complete discussion of role-based access control for Chapter 6, it is important to recognize how roles affect the provisioning process. Without roles, the workflow process must be tied to individuals. This approach is obviously untenable in an organization of any size; workflow needs roles to operate effectively.

The problem with roles is their definition. Too many vendors in the identity management market have abused the term and have made it hard for organizations to understand how to map roles to positions in their organizations. SAP, for instance, defines a role in its Human Capital Management (HCM) system as a level of access rights within the subsystem. This definition of a role has been found wanting as companies move further into the identity management area. SAP has now adopted a model in which there are "business roles" and "technical roles" as a way to ameliorate the problem.

Ideally, as Figure 5.3 illustrates, there should be a mapping of users to access rights via roles.

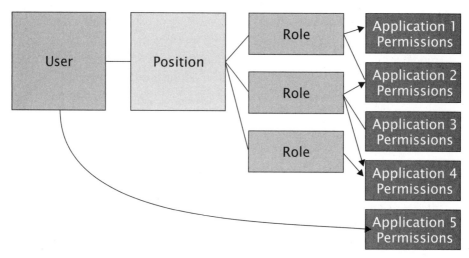

Figure 5.3: Role mapping

The degree to which a position maps to a role will vary from implementation to implementation. As far as possible, however, all access rights should be assigned via a role, and roles should be determined by positions within the organization. For instance, if someone has a position as the Operations Manager in an organization, that person might have a role called Business

Unit Manager. In the accounting system, the business unit managers might have General Ledger access and Financial Report permissions. In the HR system, there is likely a Manager of Operations role that gives access to the staff records within the Operations business unit. In the production control system, the Operations Manager might simply have Manager access rights, which give control over most production processes.

There are, however, situations in which a person requires access rights that are not connected with his or her position. For example, a business unit manager might need to have an account on the project management system. These are specific access rights that are assigned to a person and not tied to a specific role. An identity management environment with role management must accommodate this requirement for role-assigned permissions as well as the direct assignment of user-based roles even if this is on a temporary basis. A well-designed system will be able to accommodate these special cases and ensure that access rights are periodically reviewed and rescinded when no longer required. Special access rights are often required when a person moves into a new role but needs to retain some of the rights associated with the old position for a period of time while a successor is trained. A good identity system will track such assignments to ensure such permissions are disabled when no longer required.

The Benefits of Roles

Notwithstanding the problems associated with implementing roles (which we will discuss in Chapter 6), significant benefits accrue to implementing a role-based access control system. The immediate benefit is to considerably simplify the provisioning process. Rather than having to gain individual approval for every access permission to be granted to a new hire, if access permissions have been preassigned to a person's position, once approval for the position assignment has been made, access rights can be granted immediately.

Temporary assignments are similarly simplified. By way of example, consider the situation in which a company has an Operations Manager who manages the Operations Business Unit in the organization. If one of his staff is temporarily seconded to the position of Operations Manager while the incumbent is on vacation, simply adding this position to the user (within the corporate directory) will automatically grant the seconded person the appropriate access rights. Similarly, should the generic rights of a Business Unit Manager role not be appropriate for a person while that person is acting in the position of Operations Manager, simply removing this role from the position for the period of the secondment will remove the associated access rights.

De-provisioning also benefits from a role-based assignment of permissions. As soon as the person leaves the position, via a company move or an exit from the company, the position association is removed from the user and the associated access rights are rescinded.

Automating a Provisioning System

Multiple components work together to form a provisioning system:

Electronic forms package. Paper forms have no place in a provisioning system. To manually collect information that then requires a data entry step makes little sense. Not only does it incur costs (for the data entry person), but it provides an opportunity for error to creep into the identity management system. Users are generally best at spelling their own names and correctly entering their addresses, so they should perform this task. A common argument to hold onto the past and resist moving to a more efficient process is the desire to maintain consistency in the identity data store. If users are allowed to enter their own information, the argument goes, the data will be a mess; first letters of names won't be capitalized, city names won't be in upper case, and telephone numbers won't include area codes. All of these cases can well be accommodated by a good forms package that applies data masks on entry of data.

A common implementation practice is to give the user an electronic form to be completed, printed, and signed. The paper form is then maintained as a record of the person's agreement to the terms and conditions of the requested service.

If the maintenance of a hardcopy signature is really required, such a process makes sense, but the form should not be used for data entry (i.e., the data capture should be electronic at the time the form is created).

A forms package also provides the tool for data update. One of the major sources of data integrity problems is the difficulty users experience in making changes when they change address, telephone number, or bank account details. If staff members must fill in a form, find the person responsible for updating their record, or seek approval for a change, they will likely not take the time to do it. A user self-service facility is an important component of a provisioning system.

The selection of a forms package is not trivial. Some organizations mandate that an online form must look like the paper form it is replacing. In this case, a forms package with a "pixel-perfect" capability is required. While this functionality is sometimes considered mandatory, in that it simplifies the transition from the paper form to the electronic world, experience shows that the desire to maintain the look of a hardcopy form soon dissipates, and a more logical grouping of data attributes on an electronic form results.

Another issue is signatures. A forms package needs some mechanism to record who approved a form. More advanced packages accommodate digital signatures; these solutions create an electronically signed form that can be verified with the signatory's public key certificate, but this approach requires public key infrastructure (PKI) to make it work. More simple environments rely on a workflow engine that records a user's log-on ID when they approve a form. This alternative is considered sufficient for most provisioning processes.

Workflow engine. The workflow engine is the cog that makes the provisioning process work. The tool must provide the ability to manage "job queues" that collect data, manage approvals, and update data stores. These job queues must be configured to properly sequence, time, and validate workflow events. For instance, a workflow might be configured to grant access to a company's Internet service. A user wanting to access the Internet would complete the online form, which is then sent to the manager either as an email or as an email notification requesting the manager to enter the workflow system and approve or deny the request. If the manager does not do this within the prescribed time, the request can be repeated or escalated.

Data synchronization engine. In most identity management environments, besides a workflow facility there is also a requirement for a synchronization tool. This tool acts as a data pump, copying data from authoritative data sources to downstream systems (sometimes called data sinks) to avoid duplicative data entry. Data synchronization engines are sometimes called "connectors" and are typically provided by database or directory vendors for importing or exporting data.

The sophistication of data synchronization engines varies widely. In some cases, the tools are basic, simply moving data on a periodic basis from one repository to another. In other cases, a synchronization tool connects to multiple repositories and performs data transformations in the synchronization process.

Transformations change data based on a predefined set of rules as the data is synchronized from one data repository to another. A simple transformation uses a "data mask" to ensure, for instance, that phone numbers are copied into a standard format. A more complex transformation might require first name and last name from the HR system to be concatenated into a common name for a white pages directory.

Most synchronization engines that claim to be event-driven aren't. It is typically quite hard to get a directory or database to issue an instruction to the synchronization engine to cause a synchronization event. Most tools maintain a "state" database, which they periodically compare with the source repository. When a difference is detected, a write to the destination repository occurs. In this way, only delta updates (changes) are written to the destination store, not the whole database or directory.

In some cases, a synchronization engine must be able to perform a two-phase synchronization. This activity requires the synchronization tool to prepare to write data to a repository but to check the target system for currency before overwriting existing data. This capability becomes important in situations in which a database or directory entry can be generated by more than one routine or application. If a change flowing to the directory or database could have been changed by another application subsequent to a transaction being recorded, it is necessary to check the timestamp of the data record before committing the change. Most specialized synchronization engines can accommodate this requirement.

Sequential and Parallel Authorization

The workflow process described above refers to a sequential workflow: The user's request is sent to the manager and, when approved, is sent to the service desk to be actioned. This flow is very typical and is often all that is required. In other cases, the workflow can get quite complex. For instance, the addition of a staff member to a Microsoft SharePoint group may require the approval of both the manager and the owner of the group. To perform such a workflow on a sequential basis would unduly delay the process. In such an instance, it is best to send the request to both approvers concurrently. When both requests are approved, access is granted. If either approver denies the request, access is denied.

Most identity manager workflow engines have the sophistication to accommodate parallel processing requirements.

Discussion Questions

1. Make a list of the attributes a company might need to store in order to record the identities of its employees. Which attributes would typically be needed by more than one application?

2. Suggest ways in which an HR manager might be encouraged to extend the role of the HR department into managing identities rather than simply managing payroll.

3. Why is it a good idea, or not a good idea, to completely redesign an online form rather than try to make it look like the paper form it's replacing?

4. Describe the difference between a workflow engine and a synchronization tool. Why are both required in a provisioning process?

Case Study

Refer to the case study in Appendix A in answering the following questions.

1. Briefly describe the provisioning process for enrolling a student. (*Hint:* Review the applications listed in Question 2, Chapter 2.)

2. University staff need access to the Library system, the ID Card system, and the eLearning system, and they need to be in the Help Desk database. Describe how you would design a provisioning system to do this. Does your solution require a workflow engine or a synchronization tool?

3. Staff are currently provisioned in an HR system that incorporates the payroll. Associates (visiting professors and contract staff) get staff-like access rights but are not entered into the HR system because they are not issued a paycheck. How might the provisioning system be changed to make it more efficient?

4. The Staff system is basically a contacts directory that contains name, location, manager name, email address, and telephone number. Describe how you would automate the provisioning of this directory.

Chapter 6

Role-Based Access Control

At several points in this book, the topic of roles has arisen. This is because roles are such an important aspect of identity management. By now, the reader should have an appreciation of why roles are used (they provide a level of abstraction between a user and his or her access rights) and the complications involved in using them (roles are typically assigned by vendors to control access to their applications, with little regard to the company's organization chart). This chapter seeks to formalize the way in which roles can be used for access control within an organization's information technology infrastructure.

So What Is RBAC?

The intent of role-based access control (RBAC) is to connect users to resources in a managed way. Most current systems use an identity-based access control (IBAC) mechanism. These solutions operate satisfactorily in small user populations (less than 5,000 users) but quickly become expensive to maintain in large population systems (more than 10,000 users). The problem is exacerbated by the need to integrate partners, suppliers, or members of the public. RBAC provides a solution

Vendors have taken various approaches to the accommodation of access rights within their applications. For example, SAP calls access rights within its application "technical roles." SAP's NetWeaver Identity Manager is used to tie these roles to individuals in the company. The Omada Identity Manager takes a different approach, establishing "job profiles" to which the SAP technical roles are connected to this problem; it is a framework for the administration of users and the resources they want to access.

Role-based access control is the process of granting access to an organization's computer programs based on the role a person is fulfilling within the organization. A person's roles are typically tied to the person's position in the organization. In other words, a person may have multiple roles based on his or her position or job function. For example, a finance officer might have the Accounts Payable Clerk role with access to the creditor's ledger and financial reporting modules.

The basic RBAC process is:

1. Instead of managing users individually, we define roles.

2. Users are associated with one or more roles, and a role is associated with a corresponding set of access rights to resources.

3. A user's access to resources is based on the access rights of the roles to which the user is assigned.

4. Identity management administrators have to manage the access rights to only a small number of role definitions, rather than many individual user permissions.

The assignment of users to roles and system access is called *role mapping*. It is a labor-intensive activity to establish, but once completed, it considerably expedites the assignment of users to access rights.

Table 6.1 shows an extract of a typical role map.

Table 6.1: Role mapping				
User	**Position**	**Role**	**Status**	**System Account**
Jeremy Jones	Finance Officer	Accounts PayableClerk	Active	SAP_FIN_AP_JOURNAL
		Accounts PayableClerk	Active	ACC_WINDOWS03
		Finance Group Member	Active	Sharepoint_01

Table 6.1: Role mapping (Continued)				
User	Position	Role	Status	System
Helen Forbes	Finance Manager	Finance Manager	Active	SAP_FIN_AP_REPORTS
		Finance Manager	Active	SAP_FIN_AR_REPORTS
		Finance Manager	Active	SAP_FIN_GL_REPORTS
		DepartmentMgr	Active	ACC_WINDOWS01
		Finance Group Member	Active	Sharepoint_01
Paul White	HR Manager	HR Manager	Active	SAP_HCM_PAYROLL
		HR Manager	Active	SAP_HCM_REPORTS
		DepartmentMgr	Active	ACC_WINDOWS01
		HR Group Member	Active	Sharepoint_02
Amanda Smith	Executive Support	Exec_PA	Disabled	SAP_FIN_GL_REPORTS
		Exec_PA	Disabled	ACC_WINDOWS_05
		Clerical Group	Disabled	Sharepoint_07

Note that:

- The Accounts Payable Clerk role has access to the Accounts Payable journal within SAP Financials, but the Finance Manager does not, although she can print from the accounts payable ledger as well as the accounts receivable and general ledger.

- The Accounts Payable Clerk and the Finance Manager are both part of the Finance SharePoint group.

- The Finance Manager and the Human Resources Manager both have department manager roles within the Windows environment.

- The Executive Support person has access to the general ledger reporting function but has either just left the organization or is on extended leave (the account has been disabled but not deleted).

RBAC enables organizations to focus on core business requirements when defining their access management, rather than having their policies determined by technicians and the enabling technology.

Why Is RBAC Important?

The main driver for RBAC is reduced cost. This advantage eventuates primarily due to reduced cost of management of access control and associated directory administration. Related cost savings result from better asset management (including software assets) and simplified audit procedures.

Tying the granting of system access to a person's role significantly reduces the cost of provisioning systems within the organization. By disassociating persons from their system access, the need to manage individual access rights is eliminated. This means that as a person moves into and out of a position within an organization, access to the associated roles is granted and rescinded automatically. There is no need for a person to requisition system access when taking on a specific job function or when leaving a position; the system access can be automatically disabled.

Increased Productivity and Efficiency

RBAC can significantly speed the response of the organization to structural changes. As the organization chart is altered within a corporate directory, RBAC can permit associated access control changes to be enabled quickly across the organization. A simple change in the organization schema will immediately change the associated assignments. Furthermore, RBAC facilitates mapping of resources to business processes, which in turn improves the ability of organizations to optimize business processes. Whereas under an IBAC system, users must individually request access to all the appropriate systems when a business process change takes place, under an RBAC structure appropriate access is automatically granted when such a change occurs. Large reassignments, such as when a division is moved from one part of the organization to another, can be effected relatively quickly with an RBAC model in place.

As an example, let's imagine that a company moves its procurement unit from the Finance department to the Operations business unit to align the unit more closely with the work it is supporting. If all employees in Operations participate in a SharePoint group, the procurement staff will automatically be granted access to the Operations SharePoint group as soon as they are moved into the Operations directory information tree. Similarly, if they should no longer have access to the Finance system, RBAC can automatically remove these permissions as soon as the directory change occurs.

RBAC also facilitates delegation within the organization. When a manager temporarily delegates a role to a subordinate, the access rights associated with the role are quickly and easily assigned to the staff member. It is not necessary to contact the IT department to achieve the access rights change and to remember to revoke the rights at the end of the assignment.

RBAC reduces the effort required to administer users' access rights across the organization.

Increased Security

RBAC enables improved security policy enforcement. By assigning roles to group access rights, the administrator can quickly grant, and more importantly revoke, access to resources. This separation of duties and secure access rights in the end-user community significantly reduces the risk of security breaches.

Basing RBAC on an organization's structure enables the principle of "least privilege" to be enforced—users have only the privileges they require, rather than, as typically happens in a IBAC mechanism, being assigned a suite of privileges that are based on who they sit next to rather that any specific requirement of the position they fill.

RBAC also enables separation of duties (SoD). It is vitally important for organizations to control who can initiate transactions on their behalf, particularly in the finance area. For instance, the person selecting a supplier for a particular contract should not be able to enter the accounts payable subsystem and approve a payment to the supplier. This separation can be effectively accomplished only if access to the finance system is enabled via an RBAC model.

Business Visibility of Security Administration

In too many organizations, business units have ineffectual control over the policies for which they are responsible. It is the business units that should determine the security policies that impact their lines of business, and they should then monitor and manage adherence to the policy. Due to system constraints, however, administering policy often falls to the IT group, which typically lacks the requisite responsibility to act on policy violations.

RBAC affords the potential for business unit managers not only to administer the policy but also to monitor and audit adherence to it.

Speed of Response to Business and Organizational Change

Most large organizations fail to adequately manage changes in their organization chart. This situation is particularly a problem in government, where whenever the governing party changes, some reorganization in the machinery of the government occurs. Responding to change is the Achilles heel of large organizations and a source of considerable waste.

RBAC diminishes the effort required to respond to change by enabling organizations to move roles from one part of the organization to another. With RBAC in place, access controls are no longer a hindrance to accommodating organizational change.

Management of Heterogeneous Systems

A properly designed RBAC environment can also aid in the management of multiple, diverse systems. Defining a role model to which all core computer applications must adhere provides for a coherent management model that ensures that access to the various systems is both managed and logical. In such an environment, separation of duties across systems can also be monitored and managed.

Scalability

As systems grow in size, so does the importance of RBAC. For organizations with less than 5,000 staff, RBAC might be more expensive to implement than an individual access control model, but as staff numbers increase above this figure, RBAC becomes increasingly easier to justify. Beyond 10,000 staff, RBAC is mandatory for organizations seeking to control costs.

Improved Business Processes and Value-chain Efficiency

Another key advantage to implementing an RBAC environment is the benefits that accrue to business process management and value chain efficiency. At various points in a business process, it is necessary to issue advice, seek approval to proceed, or request information. Processes that refer these events to the appropriate role, rather than person, are easier to maintain and less costly to implement. In fact, the role definition stage of an RBAC implementation should map all impacted business processes so that the roles match the business requirements.

Including customers and suppliers in the role maps extends these benefits to the whole value chain. Participation by suppliers in the inventory management function, for instance, can greatly improve the management of inventory levels. Establishing access control to the inventory subsystem based on supplier roles makes access by external entities easier to manage.

Regulatory and Legal Requirements and Corporate Governance

RBAC supports traceability of administrative actions. As corporate governance becomes increasingly important to organizations, the ability to verify that the initiator or approver of a transaction was qualified to undertake the action becomes mandatory. Access to undertake a transaction will be enforced by the role-based access control mechanism, so it is important for the model to be correct and maintained.

How Should RBAC Be Implemented?

Organizations typically implement far more roles than necessary. A proliferation of roles means that the identity management environment has not been planned—it's just happened. The usual culprit is the organization's Enterprise Resource Planning (ERP) system. Such systems are usually installed by vendor contractors who simply assign roles to each access permission within the application rather than working with the organization's management to plan the role assignment and tie the roles back to positions in the company's organization chart. As a result, the ability of the access control mechanism to drive savings within the organization is reduced, and "stove-pipes" within the organization's management hierarchy are reinforced, hindering the ability of the company to gain the associated benefits the RBAC mechanism can afford. For example, if a person is a "payroll clerk," he or she will typically process the payroll. If the role is "HR information systems officer," with access permissions to the payroll facility, the person is more likely to get involved in the administration of identities within the organization.

An Australian department of education initiated a role inventory in preparation for implementing a role-based access control environment. In just the academic side (schools), more than 1,200 roles were identified. The implementers reduced this number to eight and required all school personnel to be assigned to one of these eight roles. The department enjoyed significant benefits in the first year of implementation. For instance, the end-of-year process of approving assignment of students to classes for the coming year was reduced from three weeks to three days.

How Many Roles Should There Be?

Although there is no rule to define the number of roles that should be established within an organization, a couple of "rules of thumb" can be useful.

As noted above, in some cases companies will establish nearly as many roles as there are positions. The benefits of implementing RBAC in this situation are lost. It is necessary to severely restrict the number of roles; a ratio of 1:6 or better will allow benefits to accrue. This means that there would possibly be 1,600 roles in a 10,000-person organization.

From a role management perspective, the fewer the number of roles the better. From a business process perspective, the more roles that are defined the better. The tension between these two forces should result in a reasonable number of roles that will allow benefits to accrue and permit business processes to be efficient.

How Do You Handle Exceptions?

It is impossible to accommodate all the access requirements for all personnel via role assignment only. Organizations will always need to accommodate specific requirements with the assignment of specific access rights via a separate provisioning process. The requirement for specific access rights arises when a person is assigned to a function within the organization outside the position he normally holds. This might be a temporary assignment (e.g., vacation relief) or a function that is not normally assigned to the person's position, such as a Compliance Officer role that might be assigned to the most appropriate person in the business unit.

The role exception process will typically use the organization's provisioning workflow engine and must adhere to the identity management policy of the organization.

Role Discovery

The definition of roles within an organization is fraught with difficulty and can doom an RBAC initiative to failure. Although each role mapping exercise is unique, the following steps are typical of a role discovery initiative.

1. *Collect data on each user's current access*—This step is a laborious activity that requires the log-on accounts of each user to be mapped to the user's access rights. This process can be accomplished via physical access to the user's PC or by a review of the various application directories in the organization.

2. *Define the role(s) for each user*—Roles are best defined within each user's business unit and will typically be tied to the organization chart. Knowledge of the roles each position plays within the organization is required.

3. *Document the organization's security policies*—Access permissions as defined by the organization should be documented and formally adopted by the appropriate governance body within the organiza-

tion. Policy on approval of access rights, adherence to least privilege principles, and separation of duties should be defined.

4. *Modify user's access rights to align with the policies*—A data cleansing exercise is then required to correct deviations from policy and to establish the appropriate access rights for each role.

5. *Reflect each user's role(s) in the user's authentication repository record*—The role(s) of each user can then be established in the authentication directory or database.

6. *Provisioning tool deployment*—Once the infrastructure with the roles and associated assignments is in place, RBAC provisioning can commence.

A Word of Caution

Many implementations of RBAC have suffered from making the definition of roles complicated and onerous. Indeed, it is very easy to become so overwhelmed by defining relationships between persons within and external to the organization that the activity can grind to a halt and eventually get relegated to the "too-hard basket." It is strongly recommended that the entity diagrams be put away initially and a basic role map be generated showing a generally agreed-on, high-level list of roles within the organization; positions from the organization chart should then be mapped to these roles. Over time, the role map will expand, and the information architect can generate a proper relationship map that shows the extent of the relationships each role maintains.

Discussion Questions

1. Why might the implementation of an RBAC system in a smaller company (less than 5,000 staff) be more costly than managing access control individually? In the absence of an RBAC model, what tools might be employed to assist in the management of access rights for individuals?

2. Explain how the use of roles enables an organization to achieve adherence to a separation of duties policy.

3. Why do vendors installing applications with access control lists typically define more "roles" than positions?

4. Who of the following should typically assign roles within an organization? Explain your answer.

   • Vendor of the enterprise resource planning software

   • HR department

   • Individual business units

5. How does the adoption of an RBAC model enhance the de-provisioning task?

Case Study

Refer to the case study in Appendix A in answering the following questions.

1. Each faculty has its own document repository system. Each faculty also has a hierarchy of positions:

   • Dean

   • Associate Dean

   • Head of Department

   • Professor

   • Associate Professor

   • Adjunct Professor

   • Teaching Fellow

   • Research Fellow

   • Research Assistant

   These roles are not mutually exclusive. A Head of Department will typically be a Professor. An Associate Professor could be an Associate Dean. Access rights in such systems as the Library and eLearning systems will vary depending upon these positions.

   What roles might you establish for faculty members in the university?

2. Within the student body, would there be a need for roles? Why or why not?

3. While the main provisioning system accommodates provisioning into the AD authentication directory, in some cases faculty members need access to specific-purpose Unix systems in their faculty—for instance, to support research initiatives. Would you use role-based access control for these systems? Explain why or why not.

Chapter 7

Single Sign-on and Federated Authentication

Single sign-on (SSO) is a feature of an information system that lets a user log in once and gain access to multiple software systems without being prompted to log in again.

Since the dawn of computer information systems, end users have requested single sign-on because they dislike having to remember different credentials for different systems and applications. IT departments also want SSO because it decreases administrative costs significantly. SSO reduces password-related administration work and simplifies application development and support by handling authentication on a centralized rather than a per-application basis. SSO also enhances security and compliance for enterprises by providing a central facility to log system and application access.

From an end-user point of view, SSO is a much sought-after facility because it requires users to remember only one set of credentials—usually a user ID and password—to log in once and be able to access resources on multiple systems. However, achieving this "nirvana" for users is not simple from a system perspective.

The challenge is how to pass the signed-on status among different systems and applications, especially when they are operating on different platforms.

An organization might have a network log-on via Novell's eDirectory, a Lotus Notes email system on a Domino server, a mainframe application that uses Resource Access Control Facility (RACF), and SharePoint groups on Active Directory. In some cases, SSO is required between each of these different platforms.

Single Sign-on for the Enterprise

Fundamentally, there are two ways to achieve SSO across an enterprise:

- Central storage of user names and passwords for each of the supported applications

- Passing of user sign-on statuses between applications

ESSO

The first method, often referred to as *enterprise single sign-on (ESSO)*, stores the user ID/password pairs of all systems and applications in a secure "vault" within the identity management environment. Once the user has logged on to the SSO system, whenever he or she needs to access an application, the SSO system automatically performs log-in to the respective system on the user's behalf by retrieving the corresponding user name and password from the vault.

Popular Web browsers such as Firefox and Internet Explorer provide this type of SSO feature. However, browser-provided SSO supports only Web-based applications. To support disparate application types, including Web applications, client/server applications, and network operating system sign-on, the solution is to install a sign-on agent (software) at each end user's workstation. The client-side software remembers and intercepts all log-on screens for all applications, retrieves corresponding user name and password pairs from a central security vault, and performs sign-on for the end user.

The advantage of this type of ESSO is that there is no need to modify applications as they are brought into the SSO environment. ESSO does have some drawbacks, though:

- Applications still need to maintain application passwords.

- The ESSO system must be populated with the user name and password pairs for each application. When an application's password expires, this process must be repeated, which can be frustrating for end users, particularly when password expiration isn't synchronized across applications.

- The ESSO system must perform log-in smartly on behalf of the user when an application prompts the user to log on. This operation is sometimes technically unachievable if the application doesn't work the way ESSO expects. In some situations, there is no way for the ESSO system to tell when an application is prompting for a log-in. For example, in some cases the ESSO system must be configured to expect a log-in prompt after a certain time period (e.g., two seconds) once the user starts the application. If the application's performance slows due to environmental issues and the log-in prompt takes longer to be issued (e.g., five seconds), the ESSO auto log-on will fail.

- Different workstations with different operating system versions and different configurations make ESSO implementation problematic.

- Sometimes ESSO system fails to support *single sign-off*, possibly leaving sessions active when a user logs off the workstation.

SSO Sessions

The second method for achieving SSO is to save and update the user's log-on state and pass this state to those applications to which a user requests access. Once a user is logged in, the SSO system creates a user session. As long as this log-on session is valid, the user can access all applications to which he or she has access rights. To support this SSO mechanism, applications must be "SSO aware." In other words, they need to be enabled to read user session information.

Unfortunately different SSO session schemes have been developed and are in use within the industry. Popular mechanisms supported today include Kerberos (a network authentication protocol that lets individuals communicating over a non-secure network prove their identity to one another in a secure way), Central Authentication Service (CAS, a single sign-on protocol for the Web), Java Authentication and Authorization Service (JAAS, a Java security framework for user-centric security to augment Java code-based security), OpenSSO, and federated SSO based on Security Assertion Markup Language (SAML).

Single sign-off is supported naturally using the SSO session approach because the SSO system simply removes or disables the user's log-on session once the user logs off. Access to all applications and systems will therefore be prohibited.

The main advantage of this type of SSO is a more robust authentication environment that is not open to the vagaries of application changes. The main drawback is that this method is more difficult to deploy. Despite this fact, SSO sessions have become the mainstream approach today, and their implementation is becoming easier as systems vendors and application developers embrace open standards.

Table 7.1 provides a high-level summary of the development of SSO and its relationship to standards.

Table 7.1: SSO summary				
Period	Mainstream SSO standards	Mainstream communications protocols	Mainstream systems	Mainstream SSO methods
1960–1989	None	DECnet, SNA, TCP/IP, and others; presentation-layer protocols: 3270, 5250	Different hardware, different platforms; proprietary client-side applications	SSO supported only within a single-vendor environment
1990–1999	Kerberos	Same as above	Standardized client-side platforms (Windows 95/98/2000); proprietary client-side applications	ESSO, SSO using particular SSO scheme
2000–2009	CAS, Kerberos, SAML	HTTP/HTML, SAML, SOAP, TCP/IPv4	Standardized client-side platforms (Windows XP/Vista); standardized client-side application (HTML browser)	Web SSO, ESSO

Integrated Windows Authentication

In many organizations, employees log in to the Microsoft Windows network operating system before accessing other applications. In such a scenario, SSO can be achieved by trusting the Windows log-on session. For example, if Microsoft Outlook is the client and Microsoft Exchange is the server, users can simply start and use Outlook without having to log on to Exchange first. Applications in such an environment can provide SSO simply by reading and trusting the user's Windows log-on session. In Microsoft's world, enterprises can provide SSO easily if their applications and infrastructure follow Microsoft's Windows domain framework. This method is called Integrated Windows Authentication.

Web SSO

Web single sign-on is gaining importance today as enterprises move away from client/server configurations toward a Web services infrastructure. Under the Web SSO model, Web-based applications—running on different application servers—can share the same log-in environment, which means users are not continually prompted for the user name and password as they move from application to application.

For example, consider the case of a hotel where guests can book time on the hotel tennis court. Web SSO would let guests reserve the court through the hotel's main Web site, to which they would first authenticate. In the background, the hotel site would pass the user's logged-in state, together with the necessary information, to the tennis court booking application. The Web site would recognize the guest as a valid user who will be staying in the hotel on certain days; it therefore could approve the tennis court booking and add the court costs to the guest's hotel bill.

Here's how this works internally. Every Web browser has a persistence layer that stores session detail and temporary data in HTTP *cookies*. A Web SSO system creates a cookie that represents the user's log-in state or log-in session. The HTTP protocol standard requires that every HTTP request sent from a browser to a Web server include relevant cookies stored in the browser memory. The Web SSO system uses these cookies to validate users' log-in sessions. Such cookies are known as *session cookies* because they persist only for the duration of the session.

Furthermore, because all Web-based applications use the open-standard HTTP/HTML presentation layer protocol, the Web SSO system can intercept and alter the HTTP messages communicated between the browser and the application's Web server. The HTTP header portion of the HTTP message is thus used to provide additional SSO information (e.g., the name of the authenticated user) to Web applications.

The Use of Proxies and Agents

As described above, Web SSO systems require an interceptor sitting between the user's browser and the application's Web server. Basically, Web SSO uses two common architectures: a proxy-based architecture and an agent-based architecture.

The formal term for the interceptor is *policy enforcement point (PEP)*. A PEP can be an agent installed as plug-in to the Web server filtering all HTTP traffic. It can also appear as a separate process (e.g., a separate physical server) intercepting all HTTP traffic between the Web servers and the user's browser. In the latter case, the Web servers must be configured so that they will permit HTTP requests coming only from the PEP proxy. This kind of proxy server is called a *reverse proxy server*.

Even though the communications between the browser, the Web SSO system, and the Web server typically use Secure Sockets Layer (SSL) technology, hackers have been able to apply *replay attacks*. In this type of assault, a piece of hacking software installed on the client's workstation intercepts and copies HTTP messages sent from the browser to the Web server. The user's session cookie is also copied and is used to send HTTP requests from the hacker's server with the valid cookie. To minimize secure session hijacking:

- Implement session time-out to reduce the life span of session cookies.

- Require users to provide additional credentials, such as a one-time password.

- Restrict access to specific workstations equipped with uniquely identifiable hardware (e.g., a Trusted Platform Module, or TPM).

- Require users to authenticate via a token, such as a certificate stored on a smartcard.

Some Web SSO systems can support PEP agents and PEP proxies at the same time. Each PEP usually talks to a central server called a *policy decision point (PDP)* server. The PDP, in turn, communicates with back-end directory servers to authenticate and authorize users' requests.

In a Web SSO environment, applications need to be "Web SSO aware." A common approach requires the applications to obtain a user's particulars by reading the HTTP header information inserted by the PEP module. Web applications trust the Web SSO system, meaning if requests do come in, they are assumed to have been validated. In some cases, certain Web applications cannot be modified and therefore cannot read HTTP header information to identify the user and obtain other user information. In such cases, the Web SSO system needs to support automatic log-on. The method is similar to ESSO except that the form-fill action (i.e., supplying the user ID/password to a log-in form on behalf of the end user) is performed at the server end. Only PEP proxy can support automatic log-on at the server end.

Figure 7.1 shows a Web SSO configuration that includes both a PEP agent and a PEP proxy.

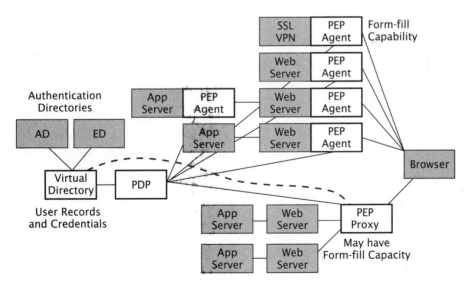

Figure 7.1: Web SSO

The advantage of agent-based architecture is the reduced need for additional hardware to host the PEP proxy server and to use Web server excess CPU power and/or memory. The advantage of proxy-based architecture is it reduces the issue of compatibility considerations between PEP agents and the corresponding Web servers.

Specific PEP modules can be developed to protect different types of resources, such as Java 2 Platform, Enterprise Edition (J2EE) application server resources; Web services; and SSL virtual private network (VPN) appliances. Web SSO systems usually provide an application program interface or software development kit for such customization needs.

In a Web SSO configuration such as the one shown in the figure, a proprietary SSO communications protocol between the PDP and PEP is typical, but it is now possible to use open-standard Security Assertion Markup Language (SAML) to achieve the same result. With SAML, the architecture can be extended to multiple enterprises and essentially becomes a federated SSO environment. Although the use of the SAML standard for enterprise-level SSO is growing, it still is not widely deployed. In the case of cross-domain SSO (i.e., SSO between different Internet domains), a proprietary scheme remains the norm. The reason why cross-domain is significant is because in the HTTP world, cookies (i.e., user sessions) can be read only by servers sitting in the same domain.

Some enterprises would like to provide SSO to users shortly after they log on to the Windows network operating system. In such cases, the SSO system must provide a way to send the Windows log-on state to the Web SSO environment. Microsoft provides a way to achieve this through its Internet Information Services (IIS), a set of Internet-based services for servers used with Windows.

A Word About Policy Enforcement

The PDP module of a Web SSO system performs policy enforcement. Policies control how resources are accessed via the imposition of *rules*. The following are some examples of policy rules:

- Users accessing resource A must be authenticated with authentication level 2.

- Users accessing resource A must log in again.

- Only managers can access resource A.

- Resource A can be accessed only during office hours.

It is the job of the PEP agent, or the PEP proxy, to enforce compliance with these rules, while the PDP module evaluates the rules by assessing user data, including the user's particulars and roles, environment information, and, most important, the authorization policies.

Federated Authentication

The premise of any identity management environment is that someone is going to manage the identities, an activity that can be extremely time-consuming and onerous. You have to make contact with each person, collect and verify the person's details, store those details, and assign access rights—and then the person moves house!

Keeping track of people and making sure the data you store about them stays current is an ongoing and expensive undertaking. What if you could get someone else to do it? If it's doctors who access your system, why not let the medical board maintain each doctor's details? If it's travel agents, how about having the travel agent association maintain the identities? If it's taxi drivers who access your site, shouldn't the licensing board for taxi drivers maintain their identity records?

This is where *federated authentication* comes into play. In a federated authentication environment, the most logical organization to maintain identities does just that, and service providers trust the credentials provided by these organizations.

A federated authentication environment includes *identity providers (IdPs)* and *service providers (SPs)*. The identity providers are the associations or certification bodies that agree to attest to their members' identities;

furthermore, individual members can control the identity details they want an identity provider to release to each service provider.

An organization providing a service that requires users to be authenticated accesses the identity provider and obtains the credentials of a user requesting access to the service. These credentials are compared with the service request, and if the user is satisfactorily authenticated, the service is provided.

In the tennis court booking example discussed previously, it would be desirable to let guests pre-book the court through the hotel's Web site simply by entering the hotel Web site without log-in because they have logged in to the travel agency Web site from which they booked the hotel room in the first place. In the background, the travel agency Web site passes the guest's logged-in state, together with the necessary information, to the hotel Web site. The hotel site thus knows that the person is a valid user who will be staying in the hotel on certain days, and it therefore can approve the tennis court booking.

Given its significant benefits, why is federated authentication not more prevalent in business today? Organizations are undoubtedly moving toward greater federation; what's surprising is how long it is taking.

Part of the reason for the slow adoption is the inherent level of distrust that can exist between entities doing business; if I am an insurance company, do I trust insurance agents who access my quotation systems to always act with integrity? Another issue is the difficulty in assigning costs; in other words, who will pay for the technology? If I must modify my systems to accommodate federation, should that be at my cost?

Fortunately, these issues are gradually being resolved, and over the next few years we can expect to see extensive and significant federated authentication environments.

The Components: ID Providers and Service Providers

As noted, the two main components of a federated authentication environment are identity providers and service providers.

Identity providers, as the name implies, are solely responsible for providing data attesting to the identities of the people or organizations in their identity store. They must be able to determine which service providers can request identity information from them and must decide on the identity detail that they can release on the identities in the store.

Service providers can be a variety of entities. In some cases, they provide application services whereby users access an application over the network—Software As a Service (SaaS) providers fall into this category. Service providers may also be document repositories from which users can gain access to documents, or they may be third-party providers operating a facility such as a payment service.

In the example depicted in Figure 7.2, the service providers do not need to maintain identity stores. This is a major benefit for the service providers, relieving them of an onerous and costly activity. Equally, the use of an identify provider gives the user much better control over the identity data to be released to prospective service providers. In the example, the identity packet provided to each service provider can be different.

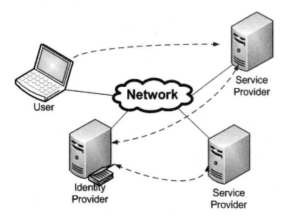

Figure 7.2: Federated authentication

WAYFs and Other Things

The obvious question becomes "How does the service provider know what identity provider to contact for identity information when a user accesses a service?" There are several ways this is done; in the commercial world, the service provider often determines the IdP from the email address of the requesting party. Although this approach works well within a closed user group, it is less practical in a federated environment open to a wide, potentially global, environment.

A useful model for widespread deployment of federated authentication is being implemented in the academic world. In academia, it is often necessary to grant access to services to users from other educational institutions, sometimes on a global basis. It makes little sense for a university in the United States to maintain identity data for personnel in an Australian university. A better solution is for the American university to trust the Australian university's identity management and grant access to its systems based on a successful authentication from the Australian university's identity provider.

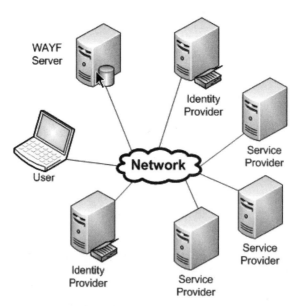

Figure 7.3: "Where are you from" server

Academics have therefore adopted a "where are you from," or WAYF, server configuration to which service providers can apply to identify the identity provider they should be using to authorize a service request from a remote user. Figure 7.3 shows a sample WAYF configuration.

What Are the Pitfalls?

Two main issues arise with federated authentication: trust and standards. First, the identity providers and the service providers must trust each other. There are multiple situations in which a service provider may grant access to its application or document store; these must fit the user profiles being maintained by the respective identity providers. The service providers must also be satisfied that the identity provider has appropriate mechanisms in place to remove an identity from the data store when the identity is no longer eligible to receive the service.

The second major issue is the adoption of standards. The adoption of standards is critical to federation. The most important one is the *Security Assertion Markup Language* standard. SAML is used to transport identity credentials between an identity provider and a service provider. The SAML standard has undergone several revisions, and it is important for computer applications to support the revision appropriate for the identity service(s) they are using. It is also important for the federation to agree on the message contents.

Although SAML adequately provides for the transport of identity credentials, the identity provider and service provider must agree on the format of credentials being supplied. In other words, the credentials being provided by the identity provider must be understood and must be appropriate for the access required at the service provider. In the academic environment, *Shibboleth* is one such credentialing mechanism. Shibboleth is an open, standards-based approach that permits sharing credentials within a community. It is used heavily within the academic community to pass authorization credentials between the participants in the federation.

It is also necessary to agree on the names for the attributes being supplied in a SAML message. In academia, LDAP directories use the eduPerson extensions to the inetOrgPerson schema. This schema defines the names of the attributes being stored in the identity repository. For instance, under this schema all systems agree that an attribute called eduPersonAffiliation will contain the name of the user's university. It is interesting to note that the Australian Access Federation (AAF) has defined further extensions under a schema called auEduPerson.

All major suppliers in the identity management sector now provide a federation solution. We will see more and larger deployments over the next few years.

Discussion Questions

1. What are the two main single sign-on (SSO) methods, and when might you use each method?

2. Why is Web SSO easier to use than enterprise single sign-on (ESSO)?

3. What are the decision points in selecting a proxy server or agent Web SSO solution? Would the number of workstations in the organization or the number of Web-based applications have a bearing on the decision as to which method to use?

4. What are the major factors hindering the deployment of federated authentication?

Case Study

Refer to the case study in Appendix A in answering the following questions.

1. Both the Oracle Financials and the Staff database have a Web front end. Explain how a Web SSO environment could be of benefit in this environment.

2. The university has a stated preference for deploying externally hosted applications rather than deploying and managing applications on the university's infrastructure. What problems arise in authenticating staff and students in an externally hosted environment? Can a federated authentication help or not?

Chapter 8

Governance, Risk, and Compliance

The genesis of the term GRC—Governance, Risk, and Compliance—is lost in antiquity, somewhere in the late 20th century. Companies such as IBM and SAP latched on to the phrase to spread a little FUD—Fear, Uncertainty, and Doubt—and to indicate how their tools help customers to make sense of what they consider a complex subject.

In reality, all organizations have a governance framework, they all undertake risk management, and they all set policies to which they measure compliance. The real issue is better stated as "Are the policies and processes by which we measure conformance satisfactory, transparent, and repeatable?"

To be fair, organizations are increasingly confronted with stiffer regulatory compliance requirements as a result of spectacular failures in recent times. The Enron debacle of 2001, followed closely by the WorldCom collapse, spawned a number of initiatives, such as the Sarbanes-Oxley legislation and the Health Insurance Portability and Accountability Act (HIPAA) regulations in the United States. The global meltdown of the financial markets in late 2008 exacerbated the increasing imposition of regulation, and the financial sector suffered the imposition of audit and control requirements.

Governance is the ability of a company's management to establish the policy and implement the processes by which the organization will be managed. It will encompass the requirements of the board of directors, shareholders, industry ombudsmen, and government regulators.

Risk management involves the identification, analysis, and response mechanisms to the risk events that the organization faces. It is not only a defensive operation to minimize the effect of a risk event; it is also proactive, ensuring that the organization is ready to take advantage of the triggering of a risk event.

Compliance is the process of ensuring that the governance policy is met. It requires a level of monitoring, analysis, and reporting.

These three elements are intricately tied to the management of identities. Governance policies will establish who can get access to which functions in the organization and the conditions that are imposed on that access. For instance, the same person should not hold the procurement officer role and the accounts payable clerk role; in other words, the person sending a purchase order to a supplier should not be able to approve the payment for that order.

Risk management must identify who is responsible in the event a risk is triggered.

Compliance must monitor who performs transactions and must report on any policy violations. If the purchasing officer tries to place an order in excess of his or her financial delegation, the system must identify this fact and notify the appropriate authority.

With increased focus on governance, auditing and reporting are critical to a "best practice" identity management environment. Indeed, it is not possible to initiate a compliance regime without a robust identity management infrastructure.

The components of such an identity management framework are threefold:

- Strict controls on access rights based on HR records

- Definition of and strict adherence to business policies to govern identity management

- Robust system cleansing and auditing procedures

HR Pattern-based Auditing

Pattern-based auditing is a mechanism to identify and list suspicious users, roles, and resources. This mechanism is based on HR patterns analysis or an analysis of the patterns of privilege assignment. The assignment of privileges enables access to company resources. The analysis of transactions uses patterns to identify potential fraudulent activity. Pattern-based auditing typically looks for anomalies within user accounts, roles established in the identity management system, or unusual patterns of use.

A common audit requirement is to report on accounts that have no tie-back to the organization's identity store(s). These could be accounts that have been left active when their owners exit the business, or they might be generic accounts established for system administration purposes (i.e., they do not have a single user).

Auditors also will review situations in which similar roles may exist in a single authorization store. Roles with similar names and/or positions in the role hierarchy may indicate that duplicate roles have been established by mistake or for fraudulent activity.

In some cases, resources such as routers or systems will have multiple entries in an authentication data store. Bogus resources might have been established for fraudulent activity.

Odd patterns of use can also indicate suspect activity. Persons with an unusually high number of sessions, or resources with an unusually low number of connections, may indicate fraudulent activity.

The various search types analyze the different objects by discovering patterns based on users' HR attributes, resource attributes, and access rights.

An HR pattern-based audit can also suggest changes that can be made to a configuration to simplify the role model. There may be an opportunity to collapse similar roles into one, to remove redundant roles, or to establish a role hierarchy that simplifies assignment of access rights to users.

A word of caution: The meaning of terms such as user, role, profile, permissions, and resource can change from system to system. For example, in Active Directory, groups are akin to roles, and there is no opportunity to expand the role hierarchy beyond the groups. In IBM's Resource Access Control Facility (RACF), roles are groups and resources are DataSets. SAP systems use two kinds of roles: business roles, which equate to functions within the SAP module, and technical roles, which equate to access permissions. It is important for everyone to agree on the use of these terms whenever discussing identity management; it is easy for a vendor and a customer to have a lengthy discussion regarding a product solution with neither fully understanding the other.

Pattern Reporting

An auditor who inspects access rights or privileges is generally looking for various situations:

- *Orphan accounts (accounts with no HR data)*—In most systems, there are accounts that are assigned to persons as well as generic accounts used for activities such as system administration. For accounts assigned to a person, the auditor wants to see whether any active accounts belong to users who have left the company. The auditor typically makes this determination by correlating the accounts from the target system with the HR database and finding any accounts that exist in the target system and cannot be matched to active entries in the HR system.

- *Accounts with no links to roles and/or resources*—There may be accounts within the target applications that are not being used any more. They are not linked to any group or to any resource. This is bad practice, and such accounts should be removed.

- *Suspect user–resource connections*—Links between a user and a resource that are out of the norm—in other words, the user's HR attributes are not aligned with other users who have access to the same resource—may indicate a fraudulent activity.

- *List of potential "collectors"*—Collectors are users who were badly managed when their HR attributes were changed and thus retained their old access rights. Most provisioning systems have mechanisms to minimize the likelihood of this situation occurring by using *provisioning rules*. For instance, a rule might be "Title=Clerk"; if the user is promoted to Finance Officer, the clerk access is removed. Such rules ensure that only users who meet the rule or criteria can access the associated resource. This design simplifies the management of access rights for staff who change roles.

- *Suspect user–group connections*—Certain links between users and groups are suspicious because a user's HR attributes are very different from other users who have access to the same group.

- *Dual user–resource link*—In this instance, a user is linked to a resource both via his or her role and directly from the HR record.

- *Dual role–resource link*—Sometimes, a user may be linked to a resource via two different groups, or one group may be a member of another that also has access to the resource. This configuration is bad practice.

- *Multiple accounts*—A single person may have more than one account. Although this practice is quite prevalent in legacy systems, it is not a good idea.

- *Similar roles and role hierarchy*—Unless roles are managed properly, they can get out of hand, with a role becoming a sub-role of another role. Not only is this situation confusing, but it can lead to the inability to properly identify separation of duties (SoD) violations. Properly managing roles is an important component of any identity management environment.

- *Groups for almost the same resources*—The existence of two groups with similar access patterns indicates a poorly managed system that possibly has too many roles/groups connected to the same resource. In this case, it is likely that the roles can be merged and the provisioning rule updated to reflect the new roles.

Business Policies (IT Controls and SoD Rules)

All organizations have a set of business policies. For instance, it is likely that only employees above a certain rank can submit a report to the management board, only the public relations manager can issue a press report, only a procurement officer can issue a purchase order, and so on. Organizations need a set of rules that addresses these policies and applies the associated restrictions. IT systems are increasingly being called upon to enforce these policies and assist in reporting on adherence to them.

IT systems can apply rule-based policies using roles and access rights to enforce business process rules defined by the lines of business within the organization. Rules typically fall into one of four categories:

- *Association of roles to resources*—Example: The plan plotter can be accessed only by users in the Engineering role.

- *Association of user attributes to roles/resources*—Example: All users must belong to at least one role.

- *Segregation of duty between roles and resources*—Example: An Accounts Payable clerk cannot be a Purchasing Agent.

- *Limits on role or resource use*—Example: Only one concurrent session can be established to the production control system at one time.

Policy rule editors typically use a wizard to enable a user to create, edit, or print out rules. Some tools also have the ability to import many restrictions from comma-separated files and generate reports that display the restrictions in a restriction table, such as the one shown in Table 8.1.

Table 8.1: Sample restriction table				
	Finance Branch	HR Management	Line of Business	Corporate Services
Finance role				
HR role	X		X	X
LoB role	X	X		
Corporate role		X		

The simplified matrix shown here indicates that someone in the Finance branch is not allowed to hold a role with access to the HR system or a line-of-business (LoB) function, such as a system that is used in one of the business operations. Similarly, someone in the HR Management branch must not have access to an operational system or a corporate function, such as performance reporting.

Best Practices for System Cleansing and Auditing

When a company starts to establish a robust identity management environment, one of its first activities will be data cleansing. Invariably, the company will be dealing with identity repositories in a variety of directories, databases, and applications that contain old data, names that are spelled differently, and generic accounts that should not be used.

Before starting a cleansing and auditing project, it is wise to define the problems that the organization is facing in order to manage the access rights to computer resources. Reference to the business rules discussed earlier is necessary to observe internal and external restrictions and regulatory requirements. This information will help prioritize the cleansing and auditing tasks.

System administrators will be challenged by the following issues and will likely need to acquire tools to help with the system analysis and produce reports. The system administrator must analyze the target system to identify the following information:

- The number of dead accounts

- The number of old roles

- The number of roles that have exactly the same users, or an overlapping set of users

- The number of roles that provide access to exactly the same transactions or data sets

- The number of users who have direct access rights to transactions (i.e., not via a profile), and the number of direct links each user has

- The number of users who have "dual access" rights to transactions (i.e., via a role as well as directly)

- The number of users who have out-of-pattern privileges to roles or direct access rights (i.e., users who have moved to a new job but retain old access rights)

Most business operational systems have built-in rules that are used to govern how policy is implemented within the system. As discussed above, these rules are usually embodied in access rights restrictions within the system. An auditor typically will require a report that demonstrates the level of adherence to such restraints.

An auditor also will likely ask for the implementation of additional rules, such as segregation of duties and other constraints on the assignment of privileges, especially to sensitive and high-risk transactions and data. Do you want to automatically verify that these rules are upheld and be able to easily provide a report that proves so?

Industry benchmarks indicate that an initial audit activity will identify problems as follows:

- Dead accounts: 5 percent to 15 percent

- Dead transactions: 10 percent to 40 percent

- Overlapping profiles: 30 percent

- Users who have direct access rights: 50 percent

- Users who have out-of-pattern access rights: 20 percent to 40 percent

Once this initial analysis has been completed, data cleansing is the next step on the way to designing and implementing a role-based access control framework and establishing and managing a governance, risk, and compliance management framework across all the company's technology platforms.

Sample Graphs

The initial analysis as described above typically takes three to five working days. The business data from a couple of major systems, such as the Active Directory repository, RACF database, and SAP account management, are compared against a file from the HR system.

The audit report will provide a good "picture" of the security situation and enable management to take the right next steps. In this section, we look at some examples of the audit analysis.

The pie chart shown in Figure 8.1 depicts the links analysis in a role-based identity management system or a mainframe application such as IBM's RACF or CA's Top Secret.

- The *Direct Links* portion of the chart represents the links between users and resources that are not driven via a role.

- The *Role Base Links* portion represents the links between users and resources via roles only.

- The *Dual Links* portion represents the direct links between users and resources that are also covered by roles.

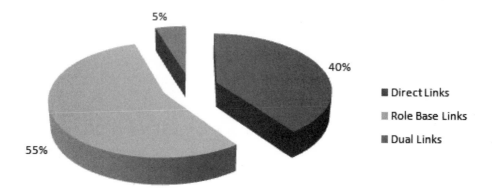

Figure 8.1: User links analysis

The Suspected Users Analysis (Figure 8.2) shows the following:

- *OK*—Percentage of users who do not have suspected access rights.

- *Suspected*—Percentage of users who have one or few suspected access rights.

- *Collectors*—Percentage of users who have many suspected access rights. Collectors are a result of bad management of "movers."

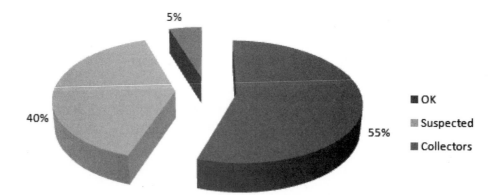

Figure 8.2: Suspected users analysis

The overlapping roles analysis shows the percentage of resources (or users) that are overlapping between roles. The sample analysis shown in Figure 8.3 represents roles that are overlapping by resources:

- 10 percent of the roles are overlapping by 100 percent, which means that they have the same resources (provision the same resources).

- 20 percent of the roles are overlapping by 90 to 99 percent, which means that 90 to 99 percent of the resources assigned to these roles are the same.

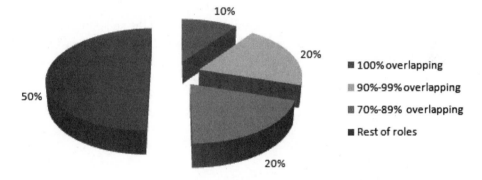

Figure 8.3: Overlapping roles analysis

Table 8.2 provides details for two overlapping roles: Finance Role A and Finance Role B. Each role has 10 resources, but the roles are overlapping by nine resources, or 90 percent. The owner of the roles or the security administrator may consider merging these roles if applicable.

Table 8.2: Overlapping roles		
	Role A=Finance Role A	Role B=Finance Role B
1	GRFIN1	GRFIN1
2	GRFIN2	GRFIN2
3	AD_APP_FIN_INT	AD_APP_FIN_INT
4	AD_APP_HR_SAL	AD_APP_HR_SAL

Table 8.2: Overlapping roles (Continued)		
	Role A=Finance Role A	Role B=Finance Role B
5	GR_PROC	GR_PROC
6	GR_INVOICES	GR_INVOICES
7	GR_CHECKS	GR_CHECKS
8	AD_CLEARING	AD_CLEARING
9	AD_ADD_USER	AD_ADD_USER
10	AD_CHANGE_USER	AD_DELETE_USER

The pie chart shown in Figure 8.4 represents the total number of access rights between users and resources that were analyzed. For each category, the chart shows the percentage of links that violated the separation of duties rules. In this example, you can see that 1 percent of the transactions violated Finance SoD rules, 2 percent violated procurement rules, and so on.

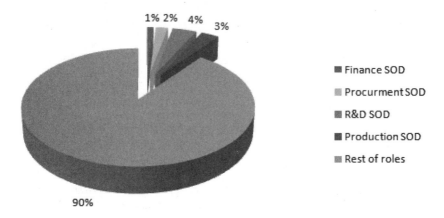

Figure 8.4: Separation of duties violations

Federated Authentication Auditing

As you learned in Chapter 7, federated authentication is becoming increasingly important as more and more organizations need to collaborate with business partners and operate in distributed environments. Federated identity technology addresses the need to identify individuals across separated security domains or businesses. Many businesses today collaborate and grant access to users from other external businesses and need to identify cross-business identities and assign resources to them. Federated authentication enables users from one business to securely access another business and the data or applications to which they are granted access.

As you can imagine, the task of governance becomes significantly more complex in a federated environment. It is difficult enough to determine who within the organization can access inventory levels; in a federated environment, external access from suppliers needs to be managed as well. It is incumbent upon those who define the identity provider (IdP) service to ensure satisfactory detail is transferred in the identity validation message to enable enforcement of SoD and other policies and to permit adequate auditing of transactions.

> A commercial insurance company in Singapore deployed a federated authentication environment to give travel agents and motor vehicle insurance agents access to prepare quotes, issue policies, and manage claims. Because no central association of agents existed to act as an authorization body, the company decided to provide the identity provider (IdP) service on its premises with a nominated manager in each participating agency. Agents' managers must provision them on the system before the agents can gain access. This deployment has significantly reduced the company's administrative work and lets it audit agent activity.

Discussion Questions

1. Why does governance, risk management, and compliance reporting have such an impact on IT? Should the IT department drive the establishment of the auditing function within a company? Why or why not?

2. If an audit finds that an unusually high number of users have both direct and role-based access to a resource, what does that indicate?

3. Prioritize the following systems according to their propensity to be subject to separation of duties (SoD) policies. Write a short paragraph to explain your reasoning.

a. Finance system

b. Human resources system

c. Production control system

d. Email system

e. Collaboration server

f. Telephone management system

Case Study

Refer to the case study in Appendix A in answering the following questions.

1. What policies might impact the university's IT systems? What SoD requirements might there be between administrative staff in the faculty and the academic staff?

2. Universities are notorious for maintaining more than one account for a single person (e.g., students who are also research assistants). What difficulties does this situation pose for policy enforcement such as SoD restrictions?

3. Would you expect there to be more audit problems on the student side or the staff side? Why?

4. The university uses Oracle Financials in a Web services environment. Where would you implement SoD policy enforcement?

5. The university plans to move the authentication store for the Oracle Web applications to the SunONE LDAP server, with a separate directory information tree for each application. Will this change help auditing of user-to-role links? Why or why not?

Chapter **9**

Implementation and Roadmap

In the preceding chapters, we discussed the various components of an identity management environment. Now, it is time to talk about strategies for implementation.

Identity management within an organization touches all facets of the information technology environment. From the initial provisioning of staff members so that they can access the company's infrastructure to the authorization of a user to conduct a business process, the identity management facility is at the core of the company's IT infrastructure.

The widespread integration of the identity management environment with almost every facet of the IT infrastructure and the organization's business processes makes implementing an identity management infrastructure a significant undertaking. An identity management environment is a long-term development that will grow and mature over several years. It is therefore important for the development to proceed in managed chunks that let the organization assimilate and take advantage of each component of the environment as it is brought online.

It might help to think of setting up an identity management environment as similar to gardening. You achieve much better results by making small adjustments over time, pruning carefully and weeding frequently, rather than letting a jungle grow and then attacking it with a machete.

A garden is but one useful metaphor. The underlying metaphor we use in this chapter likens the development of an identity management environment to the preparation for and execution of a strenuous hike. A well-prepared hiker makes good use of maps during the trip; so too does implementing an identity management environment require an overall roadmap to guide the deployment of each component. For instance, it is important for an organization to have a corporate directory to provide contact details for staff within the company. The directory must be current and accurate and will therefore depend on other components of the identity management environment, such as the provisioning workflow. The selection of the corporate directory product should thus be conducted within an overall plan, or roadmap, to ensure the directory integrates with the other components of the identity management environment.

Dividing this exercise into management "chunks" will avoid the pitfalls of implementing a large project with multiple dependencies that is highly likely to falter and never see completion. In addition, it lets the organization take advantage of the "low-hanging fruit"—those elements that will provide the highest return on investment.

This chapter discusses how to start down the road from the typical disjointed, poorly managed systems to a fully identity-enabled organization. We will review the steps to take and the stops to make along the way, and we'll note various "landmarks" you're likely to encounter during the "hike."

Getting Started

This section provides an overview of the steps that are typical when implementing an identity management infrastructure at a large organization.

Naturally, there is some work to do before beginning the implementation. You cannot start your journey until you know your current position and desired destination. The following activities are generally undertaken before an implementation begins in earnest. Either internal staff or hired specialists can perform them, depending on the organization's needs and capabilities.

Engage the Sponsor and Identify the Stakeholders

Identity management systems are costly to develop and deploy. It is therefore important that the organization is willing to commit both budget and personnel to the project. The first step, then, is to engage the right levels of the organization and make sure they share the vision of how important identity management is to the business, understand the long-term goals, and assign a budget to the initiative.

Evaluate Business Needs

The business stakeholders need to outline and prioritize the business needs for the initiative. Is the most important end goal enterprise single sign-on (ESSO), Web SSO, or federation with third parties? Maybe compliance with regulations and auditing is the top priority. Sarbanes-Oxley may require a corporate framework and toolset for tracking governance, risk, and compliance as part of an industry standard. Although it is likely that all of these are required, they cannot be delivered all at once, so the business must prioritize them so that the most important features are delivered earlier rather than later.

To correctly quantify the cost of deploying each component of the identity management environment, the IT organization will need to help in the financial analysis that forms the core of the prioritization exercise.

Evaluate the Existing IT Environment

Next, an environmental scan of the existing IT infrastructure is required to understand what is currently in place and to work out how best to integrate it with the proposed new identity management infrastructure. As noted above, the identity management environment will touch all facets of the existing infrastructure, so it is important that it is understood. This assessment should include a review of the current program of work, the projects that are already under way, and those in a pending state.

The evaluation should focus on identity—the processes currently in place to provision employees, partners, and customers. It should document the current identity stores in use within the organization and the core applications (i.e., those that will be included in the identity management environment program).

Note that only the core applications can be included in the project to ensure that the project is manageable. For smaller applications that are not included in the program, a standard interface should be provided to which smaller applications may connect if warranted.

The environmental scan should identify who manages user data (where identity data is stored), who approves accounts on the various core applications, and how access is removed when a person leaves the company.

The scan will likely identify corporate IT standards and policy decisions that need to be considered in integrating future systems into the identity management environment.

Perform Gap Analysis

Once you have documented and understand the existing infrastructure and identity processes, there will be gaps between the required functionality as prioritized by the business groups and the capability of the existing infrastructure. Document these "gaps"; this documentation will form the basis for the project work required to provide the desired identity management environment.

List and Evaluate Possible Technical Solutions

By this time, some solutions should be obvious. There generally are not too many solutions that will move the organization from the current state to the desired state. An in-depth analysis isn't required at this stage, just enough so that the team understands the broad features of the landscape of the "hike."

Risk Analysis

The project team should analyze risks based on the gaps and possible sets of solutions. This activity involves identifying and quantifying possible risks for each option as well as estimating the probability that each risk will be triggered and the anticipated cost if it is. Calculate an expected value for the risks associated with each option.

A "vendor suite" approach, in which the major components of the identity management environment are selected from the same vendor, versus a "best-of-breed" approach, whereby the products are selected from the market leader for each component, should be evaluated in this step.

Risk analysis is not a one-time activity; it will be performed continually once you start hiking. We'll discuss risk analysis in more detail later in the chapter.

Create a Roadmap

A Chinese proverb wisely advises that a 1,000-mile journey starts with a step. Deployment of a comprehensive and robust identity management infrastructure is indeed a "1,000-mile journey" and is therefore a daunting task. Many good ideas fail to see the light of day because they are interwoven with other elements that make the whole issue insurmountable.

Our metaphorical "trailhead," or starting point, requires a roadmap document that clearly indicates the overall direction and prioritizes the tasks that make up the program. At this stage, however, the roadmap is at a high level, sufficient to help the team see the main landmarks to use in navigating from the starting point to the desired goals. The details will come later.

The roadmap will also allow an initial risk analysis to be undertaken. Unlike development projects, where teams often tackle the riskiest tasks first, the roadmap should ideally include the easiest components first, and those with biggest payoffs.

Consider an RFP Process Based on Your Findings

When the team has completed its preparatory work and is armed with a realistic evaluation of the current situation, where they want to go, and the associated risks and rewards, it can consider soliciting outside advice using a request for proposal (RFP) process. We'll discuss the RFP process only briefly here because most companies have their own proprietary procedure for issuing and evaluating RFP documents.

In general, the RFP process consists of the following steps:

1. Soliciting bids from vendors and systems integrators based on stated business needs, which will include a list of the requirements and a description of the existing environment. Organizations providing proposals might also be asked to include a risk analysis to help formulate a project risk analysis.

2. Evaluation of the proposals against predefined criteria. This step typically involves "scoring" each response with an estimation of how closely the response satisfies the list of requirements.

   Comparison of the roadmap with the timeframes indicated in each response will validate the estimated program length. It also will provide insight into how realistic each responding company is and how well its ideas align with those of the organization.

   You should also conduct a separate risk analysis for each short-listed response because the risk profile will vary depending on the size and experience of each respondent.

3. At this point, a decision on the program strategy and structure is required. There may be a clear winner that offers the correct balance of technology and expertise, or you may decide to use a consortium whereby one company provides the technology and another manages the installation.

   You also need to decide whether to outsource the deployment or manage it internally. Remember that the company's identity management environment is core infrastructure and should be managed internally if possible.

Regardless of the program strategy, the company should plan to dedicate at least one employee to the project to maintain a constant voice in the process. Most vendors will insist on it.

The salient point of the entire evaluation is that the company's team and the vendor must work together as true partners.

The team is now fully assembled and it is time to plan the details of the "hike."

Create the Program Roadmap

After conducting the preceding preparatory activities, the project team will be assembled and will have a very good idea of where the organization sits with regard to the identity infrastructure and where it wants to go. The team's first activity is to assemble a detailed roadmap that will serve as the framework for the entire program's execution. We provide a sample roadmap later in the chapter.

Setting Out

Once the program roadmap is in place, the team assembles at the "trailhead" and the real journey begins. The remainder of this chapter discusses the challenges the organization is likely to encounter, provides an overview of a sample roadmap, discusses common deliverables for projects of this type, covers risk analysis, and provides a few other comments about challenges you might encounter on the journey.

Physical Implementation

The identity systems to be deployed will become core infrastructure in the IT landscape for the organization. It is therefore important to plan how these systems are to be integrated into the IT system operation once they go into production.

Although the main components of an identity management environment are at the application level (workflow tools, data synchronization engines, directories, and so on), these components, for what is essentially a mission-critical facility, must be adequately supported by a high-availability infrastructure. Directory infrastructure is quite transparent—until it fails.

It is important for the organization's approach to business continuity to extend to the identity management environment. This principle might mean implementing the various components on redundant servers with hot standbys and failover technology or, if a virtualization strategy is followed, installation of the appropriate identity management components within virtual images distributed across the organization's virtualization infrastructure.

One memorable project deliverable for a state government department was the integration of the mobility strategy with the organization's identity management infrastructure. One executive, upon seeing virtually the whole organization in his email address list, started to delete most of the entries, leaving only his personal contacts. The incorrectly configured directory connector then dutifully synchronized the changes back into the department's directory, leaving the executive's contacts as the only people capable of logging onto the network.

Typical Project Structure

As you travel from the trailhead to the various landmarks on the roadmap, each segment of the trip is typically conducted as a project on its own. These projects could be milestones in a larger program or concurrent work streams in one large project. For now, we'll assume a linear traversal of the hike's path.

As you walk a segment, you create a plan, refine requirements, fine-tune design, build, test, deploy, and assess performance. The overall roadmap can then be revised, and you can savor the view for a minute before you move on.

Each project needs to handle business requirements, technical requirements, and operational requirements (including service level agreements and ongoing support and maintenance agreements). Each project should also include its own risk assessment, so that every stakeholder can be made aware of the difficulties and challenges the team faces. This assessment also helps the project manager and staff provide realistic estimates and set reasonable schedules.

A Risk Assessment Template

An essential component of project management is the communication of the project's risk profile to the stakeholders who make up the steering committee. Each identified risk will be assigned an estimate of the following attributes:

- *Severity*—The magnitude of impact that a risk could present to the overall project

- *Likelihood*—The chance that a given risk will occur during the project

- *Risk level*—An estimation of the overall danger associated with a risk

The matrix shown in Table 9.1 depicts how the risk levels are determined.

Table 9.1: Risk level matrix			
	Likelihood		
Severity	Low	Medium	High
Low	Low	Low	Medium
Medium	Low	Medium	High
High	Medium	High	Extreme

No project should proceed with a risk in the "Extreme" likelihood range. High-level approval should be required for any "High" risk. Some form of mitigating activity would likely be required, or an insurance policy could be put in place.

A risk assessment should also include the following information for each risk:

- *Impact*—Areas affected if a given risk is realized

- *Mitigation*—Suggested actions to be taken to reduce the severity, likelihood, and/or impact of a risk

- *Risk owner*—The person responsible for ensuring that risk mitigation activity is implemented

- *Residual risk*—An adjusted risk level, in which the original risk is adjusted with the assumption that the suggested mitigations are implemented

Many project managers assign one person on the team the role of *risk officer*. This person is responsible for understanding, tracking, and, most important, facilitating the analysis of risks to the projects.

Sample Roadmap

As we noted above, the implementation of an identity management environment is a long-term, multi-year activity. Organizations therefore tend to split up the task into smaller, more manageable components and to implement each component separately. Although this approach is beneficial from a project management perspective, if it is done without an overall plan, it is likely that incompatibilities will be experienced and the full benefits of each component of the identity management environment will not be realized. The roadmap must address each of the components required within the environment, which might include the following:

- *Corporate directory*—Most organizations have a requirement for a central repository of identity data that multiple applications can use as their data store; the corporate directory will typically be a standards-based directory populated by the provisioning process.

- *Web SSO*—A single authentication environment is usually quite easy to achieve for Web services applications.

- *Enterprise SSO*—An authentication environment that accommodates the organization's core applications regardless of platform is more difficult to achieve. It normally will require synchronization between disparate data repositories.

- *Virtual directory*—In some cases, to provide a single interface for directory purposes, organizations will maintain multiple data repositories with a front end that performs real-time joins. For example, a company might need a white-pages service to provide telephone contact and location data. A virtual directory might be used to locate the person in the corporate directory, the phone number in the PABx repository, and the location in the human resources system.

- *Federated authentication*—If there is a need to authenticate persons external to the organization for access to corporate resources, a federated environment might be advisable. In this case, the organization will trust the identity management processes of an external organization to properly advise on a person's identity credentials; based on these credentials, access to the company's resources will be granted. Federation also has a part to play if an organization makes heavy use of external service providers for hosting applications. Rather than giving the external organization the company's staff details, the company can install a federated environment in which any access to the hosted applications will generate an authentication request to the organization's identity provider service.

- *Unification of authentication environments*—If an organization maintains disparate platforms (e.g., Macintosh, Unix, and Windows), it is often advisable to integrate these platforms into a single authentication environment.

- *Auditing*—Most authentication environments require monitoring and auditing to ensure policy is being adhered to; tools to provide this functionality are typically required.

The timeline for a basic roadmap might look like the one shown in Figure 9.1.

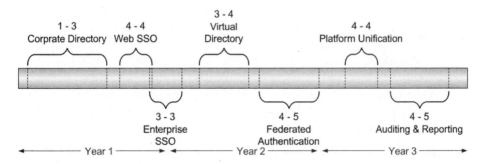

Figure 9.1: Basic roadmap timeline

The benefit to such a roadmap is that each component is seen as a part of the whole solution, in which all parts must work together. Sourcing of each component therefore occurs within the context of the complete environment. As each component is acquired and installed, these steps happen within a single environment that must integrate and work together.

Navigating the Political Landscape

As with most projects, an important determinant of success in an identity management environment is how well the project manages the political issues within the organization. As we've noted, the identity management environment pervades the whole organization, impacting staff access to core infrastructure and controlling business processes that access the identity management faculties within the organization. If the politics within the company are not managed, projects that otherwise would provide great benefit to the organization will falter and may never see the light of day. For instance, if the identity management environment requires the HR group to take ownership of the identity provisioning within the organization but HR considers its purview to be restricted to payroll administration, the implementation will falter.

> In a government entity's recent deployment planning session attended by IT resources, business process managers, and representatives from the HR branch, it was agreed that HR should drive the provisioning of access to corporate resources within the department. The HR representatives adamantly refused to take on this role because their mandate was no more than managing the payroll for the department.

Involving the Stakeholders

There is one tried and true strategy that limits political fallout: getting the stakeholders involved. If someone in the organization is included in the decision-making and implementation activity, that person is far less likely to cause grief to those performing the deployment. Such inclusion is also a good way to ensure that the identity management environment being installed is comprehensive and inclusive.

If the organization takes an enterprise architecture approach to technology planning, the impacted business units are likely to be involved in the solution planning from the early stages of the identity management planning activity. Representatives from these business units should participate in the roadmap planning workshops.

If technology planning is the purview of the IT group, a concerted effort to obtain the requisite involvement from the business units will be necessary. Failure to do so will expose the exercise to lack of cooperation at best and potential disruption at worst. Involved parties must perceive that they are integrally involved with the planning and deployment of the identity management environment. Although the IT group may initially view the inclusion of these groups as unproductive and a hindrance to the project's progress, in the long term it will expedite the process and heighten the probability that the exercise will satisfy the main business requirements.

Challenges

Several challenges are commonly encountered in an identity management program.

Budget, Budget, Budget

These programs touch so much of the organization that it is not always clear who should contribute budget to the various projects. Questions will arise about whose budget each component impacts. The program manager will need to manage the budget through the steering committee.

Consider the example of an organization adopting a Web SSO platform. The business owner of a pre-existing Web application probably didn't account for the changes that would be required to facilitate SSO. The identity management project sees the benefits of bringing the application into the SSO environment. The company will reap the benefits, but the business manager is reluctant to assign any of his budget to the activity.

As mentioned earlier, the risk profile of the project will put pressure on the project's budget. Again, the project manager will need to accommodate the expected value of the risk profile, and the steering committee will need to monitor the project's risk management in each committee meeting.

Last, because an identity management program will typically run over many years, such projects transcend the budget cycle of most organizations. This circumstance puts pressure on the program, given the rapidly changing fortunes of a business in the globalized economy.

Skilled Resources

Implementing an identity management system will likely require external specialists for many organizations. The toolsets can be complex and for specific needs, so it is likely that an organization won't have people with the necessary experience in-house. It probably would not make sense to train and maintain specialists capable of implementing the required systems because developing the requisite expertise is a long-term activity that would not be economically justifiable. We should also note that identity management experts are in demand and hence expensive to retain.

It is necessary, however, for the people who know the company's specific business processes to be involved in the project. The "experts" will depend on this knowledge.

The IT people who understand the details of a company's network and servers must also be involved in the project activity to ensure that adequate planning goes into the deployment of the identity management components. There will be a fine balance between growing internal staff and hiring external assistance.

Corporate Structure and Governance Model

By way of example of the challenges that can arise in a large-scale identity management program, consider the situation of a large U.S. company that acquired one of its competitors in France. The company's attempt to centralize its identity management facilities at its headquarters in the United States was thwarted by European Union regulations regarding privacy that prohibited the exporting of identity detail from France. The solution was to establish a distributed environment that replicated only contact detail between the two geographies.

In another instance, a large multinational company headquartered in Australia deployed a new identity management environment in conjunction with the new company portal application. The worldwide rollout proceeded smoothly until the company deployed the solution in Germany. Staff there objected to the new terms and conditions, which included a more stringent "permitted use" statement. Operations came to a stop because staff would not log into their computer systems until the statement was changed.

Managing projects across international borders with different languages and cultures is a challenge at the best of times. For an identity management project, corporate structure and governance models pose additional challenges.

Vendor "Churn"

Some organizations choose to outsource the deployment of their identity management facilities to a systems integrator chosen for its expertise in identity management. It is important that one of the evaluated project risks is the personnel assigned by the systems integrator—they will change over time. Because they are skilled resources, these individuals will be in demand and will often be deployed on new projects to get things started.

Another risk is the consolidation that's occurring in the identity management industry sector. In recent years, many of the smaller suppliers have been acquired by CA, IBM, and Oracle. It is possible that an acquisition by one of the industry conglomerates will thwart the choice of a product or team from a small boutique firm, a decision favoring agility over bulk.

The Games Vendors Play

There are several main players in the identity management space whose prime strategy is to keep the competition out. Rather than encourage an integration approach, these vendors will try to influence the solution to ensure exclusivity. Indeed, in many cases this is a wise approach. If Oracle is the prime vendor, it will often make sense to combine the Oracle Identity Manager with the Oracle Internet Directory and use Oracle's Federation Server. If the organization is aligned with Sun, the Sun Identity Manager and Sun Java System Directory Server EE make a good combination. But the customer, not the vendor, should make these decisions.

Vendors also have their own implication processes that rarely accommodate the client's real requirements. Once a vendor has been awarded an installation job, its prime task is to complete the project as quickly as possible to maximize profit on the job. Although this goal is laudable on face value, identity management implementations are complex, and any attempt to complete the projects as expeditiously as possible will compromise the solution. For instance, identity management solutions typically require the definition of job roles or profiles within the core applications. Vendors often don't want to take the time to inventory all the core applications so that the job roles can be adequately defined to accommodate all the requirements. They would rather define the roles that their application needs and leave the client to worry about the others. The roadmap approach can benefit here. If the roadmap adequately defines the complete identity management environment, the vendor should correctly scope the activity at the outset and include the necessary interfaces.

The vendor's project management capabilities are also critical in an identity management implementation.

Another game vendors play is the "I told you so" game. This is how it works: Vendors are given a portion of an implementation rather than the whole project. This situation might occur because the client wants to do some part of the project itself (to ensure control of core components of the project), or it may want to involve multiple vendors to ensure use of the "best of breed" for each component. In this case, the prime vendor may work to frustrate the project in an attempt to be given a larger slice of the overall project.

One area fraught with difficulty is data cleansing. At some point in an identity management environment project, this issue will raise its head and must be addressed.

Data cleansing is one of those activities that cannot be completed to 100 percent satisfaction. Any vendor (or customer) requiring this result will frustrate the overall project and could cause the project to be put in the "too-hard basket." The project team needs to define the level of error that is acceptable, because the closer you get to a 100 percent accurate database, the more costly it becomes. The cost of data cleansing, as Figure 9.2 shows, is *asymptotic*.

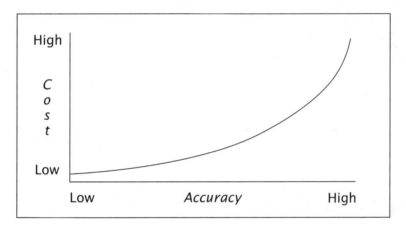

Figure 9.2: Data cleansing cost vs. database accuracy

The Importance of Project Management

The way in which an identity management project is managed will make or break it. It is important to involve an experienced project manager—one with identity management product experience. Company personnel must be included in regular team meetings, and periodic reports to the steering committee, with representatives from the stakeholders, should occur. Strict adherence to approved project control mechanisms should be enforced.

Discussion Questions

1. Name three challenges that an identity management program is likely to face. Suggest ways to lessen the impact of these challenges.

2. Should a global company use its identity management program to impose governance requirements in one region on the whole company? Why or why not?

3. What is "expected value" when calculating risk? Give an example of a risk that an identity management project might encounter, and suggest how you would calculate its expected value.

4. Compare the arguments for adopting a best-of-breed approach versus a vendor-suite approach to the acquisition of identity management components.

Case Study

Refer to the case study in Appendix A in answering the following questions.

1. Three important aspects of the university's identity management implementation are the definition of roles, the setting of policy (e.g., whether multiple identities will be allowed), and data cleansing. Suggest where these activities would come in the identity management roadmap for the university.

2. Would you recommend a suite approach or a best-of-breed approach for the university? What would be the deciding criteria?

3. How might the university mitigate the risk of churn in supplier staff over the course of the identity management program?

Chapter **10**

Public Key Infrastructure

Public key infrastructure (PKI) is a mechanism to provide

- *Digital signing of a document*, so that recipients can verify whether the originator definitely did "sign" the document

- *Encryption of a document*, to ensure that only the intended recipient can read the document

PKI achieves these security measures by using a *key pair* that consists of a publically available *public key* and a *private key* that is kept securely on the owner's PC or a storage device, such as a smartcard. A key in this context is simply a sequence of characters used in the digital signing and encryption process.

In Figure 10.1, if Bob wants to sign a document, his private key is used to generate a "signature" that is added to the file. He can then send the document to Alice, who retrieves Bob's public key certificate from the certificate server (or Bob can send Alice his certificate) and performs a signature verification process. Only Bob's public key—the other half of the key pair—can be used to verify the digital signature.

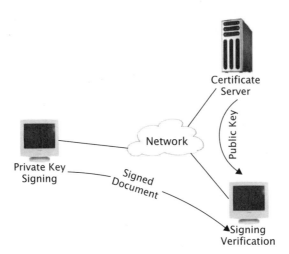

Figure 10.1: Digital signing

In Figure 10.2, Bob wants to encrypt a file so that only Alice can read it. He retrieves Alice's public key (if he does not already have it), encrypts the file (a mathematical process that generates a file that can be decrypted only by the other half of the key pair), and sends it to Alice. When Alice receives the file, she uses her private key to decrypt and read the file.

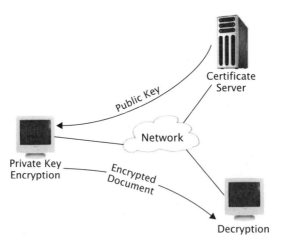

Figure 10.2: Encryption

Why Do We Need PKI?

Authentication is at the heart of online transactions. Banks want it because it eliminates "phishing." Businesses want it because it eliminates repudiation of transactions. Governments need it so that they can expand their online presence and focus on providing increased value to constituents.

Public key infrastructure was developed to enable widespread deployment of secure communications and identity management. There are two main reasons to adopt a PKI solution.

First, PKI is the only way to administer large identity management environments. Although identity management systems work well for small populations, once they exceed about 10,000 entries, they become unwieldy and the administrative overhead can prove too onerous. Password management systems with self-service facilities go some way toward alleviating the shortcomings, but there are practical limitations to the effectiveness of password management solutions for large populations.

The second reason to adopt PKI is that PKI solutions can be made far more secure than other authentication mechanisms. PKI systems are inherently more secure because they depend on the matching of two asynchronous keys. With one side of the pair always kept private, this key can be closely tied to the person (or entity) in question; when a signing or encryption event takes place, identity fraud is thus far less likely to occur. The keys are asynchronous because they are different, as opposed to synchronous systems whereby both the sender and the recipient have the same key. While the latter approach is satisfactory for encrypted communications within small populations, it is not secure enough to properly protect participants, nor is it satisfactory for digital signing.

Before the advent of PKI, secure communications systems were typically point-to-point solutions that required a high degree of management in terms of key distribution. Most installed systems today are still of this type. Although such systems are generally satisfactory in terms of the main requirement to provide encrypted communications and basic authentication, they include no mechanism to manage keys. In addition, they can be implemented only between parties that trust each other, and they are impossible to widely deploy outside closed user groups.

Public key infrastructure provides authentication, communications integrity, and non-repudiation in a public environment in which the trusting parties do not necessarily know each other. PKI also provides the ability to manage keys and therefore to control access to secure infrastructure, in real time if necessary.

How Does PKI Work?

A full PKI implementation consists of multiple components, as Figure 10.3 illustrates.

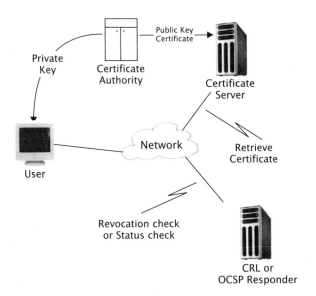

Figure 10.3: PKI components

Two main components of the infrastructure are the *certificate authority (CA)* and the *certificate server*. The CA generates the certificates that are provided to the certificate holder and to the certificate server. The certificate server contains a copy of each issued certificate, referenced by the certificate holder's relative distinguished name (RDN) and also a list of revoked certificates. These items in themselves are not expensive (depending on the "strength" required for the certificate), but they must be managed, and a level of administrative effort is necessary. The system must also be governed by policies and procedures for which some professional service expense will be required. (A certificate's *strength* is determined by the process that issues it. If a registration process puts an applicant through a 100-point check, the issued certificate is "stronger" than one based simply on a completed application form.)

The CA generates the certificates and provides them to the certificate holder via a defined process (e.g., email, courier). The private key associated with the public key must be transmitted to the certificate holder via a secure means (e.g., SSL, courier, registered mail).

When the certificate is provided to the user, it should also be written to the certificate server. Some PKI installations do not use a certificate server, but this practice is undesirable because it requires users to either carry their certificate on a device such as a smartcard or send their certificate to other participants in the scheme. The certificate server should contain a copy of each certificate in the PKI scheme and should be accessible to systems performing signature verification or document encryption. If users are part of a single organization, the certificate server should be on the organization's network; if more than one commercial entity is using the PKI, the certificate server should be available on the Internet.

Some Terminology

A lot of confusion exists over the term "certificate." A certificate is simply a small text file that contains the certificate holder's public key. As its full name implies, a *public key certificate* is totally public and can be freely copied to anyone.

The term *soft cert* refers to a certificate that resides on a computing platform, such as the user's PC. A *hard cert* is a certificate that is written to a hardware device, such as a smartcard or a USB memory stick. (The use of a smartcard or USB device for certificate storage is misleading. In actual fact, it is the private key that matters most; the certificate is written to the storage device for convenience only.)

Hardware certificates are generally considered more secure and less susceptible to fraud because they don't reside on a computer system, and the key generation process typically occurs on the device itself rather than the keys being generated externally and then written to the storage device.

How Is PKI Used?

PKI has wide application in numerous areas. Organizations can use it to provide client access to secure infrastructure or in server-side applications that encrypt sessions to public Web sites. Table 10.1 summarizes these two types of PKI technology.

Table 10.1: Server- and client-side PKI			
	Server-side PKI	**Client-side PKI**	
Typical use	Encryption of communications	Encryption of communications	Signing of transactions/documents
Authenticated entity	Originating server	Reporting entity (person or company)	Person entering transaction
Sample application	Intra-server communications	Protection of email transiting the Internet	Digital signing of a contract

Server-side PKI

Two types of communications use server-side public key technology:

- *Intra-server communications*, by which communications between networked devices are "trusted" because they are encrypted using asynchronous key pairs, essentially providing a virtual private network between the devices. PKI protocols can be used to verify the validity of a device's certificate.

- *Interactive Web server access*, in which a browser session is encrypted using a certificate on the target Web site. The user can query the certificate and decide whether to trust the site being accessed. In this instance, the server is provisioned with an X.509 certificate that a user's browser can interrogate.

We include these uses of PKI here for completeness, but they are not the focus of this chapter.

Client-side PKI

Our focus here is on the client-side use of PKI to authenticate users and encrypt communications. This purpose can be internal, such as authenticating staff for access to buildings or computer facilities, or external, such as authenticating members of the public for access to online services.

One of the major considerations in any PKI scheme is ensuring that the scheme provides sufficient security for those trusting the scheme's certificates. If the certificates are used for low-liability transactions, there is no need to require strong certificates, which typically cost more than "weak" ones. In general, the stronger the authentication requirement, the higher the liability associated with the certificates issued under the PKI scheme. The higher the certificate liability, the more complex and expensive is the legal protection required to be put in place. Organizations should avoid the cost and complexity of a PKI that exceeds actual requirements.

The Components

Let's take a closer look at the components that make up a public key infrastructure implementation.

Certificate Authority

A certificate authority (CA) issues digital certificates and maintains certificate status. A CA typically issues a certificate based on advice from a registering agent called a *registration authority (RA)*. RAs must adhere to the procedures stipulated by the CA for issuance of its certificates. The certificate practice statement (CPS) details these procedures.

Issuing Process

Although there are many variants of the process, issuing certificates typically occurs as depicted in Figure 10.4.

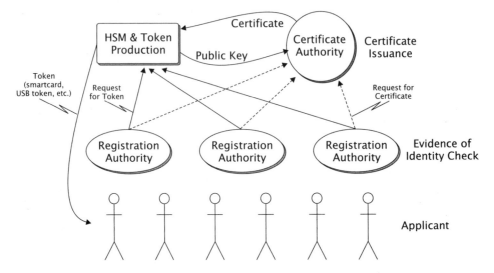

Figure 10.4: Application process

Certificates are requested at the time of the evidence of identity check (EoI). All CAs require some form of identity check before issuing a certificate; after all, they are attesting to the validity of the certificate holder's identity, so they need to be sure that applicants are who they say they are. For some CAs, this verification will be a simple check in the telephone book to make sure a person's name and address are spelled correctly. For others, it will be a 100 point check that requires sighting of a birth certificate, passport, or marriage certificate.

For large, public communities, a registration authority typically completes the EoI check, and the check is based on validation of documents that attest to the applicant's identity. In some cases, the RA will retain a certified copy of the document for CA audit purposes. The CPS will dictate these procedures.

Once the applicant has been sufficiently identified to the registration agent, he or she will typically select a personal information number (PIN) for the certificate, and the request will be sent to the certificate authority, which will generate the key pair and issue a digital certificate for the applicant. Key generation will typically occur in a hardware security module

(HSM), which might also be used to store the key pairs that it generates. Note that the digital certificate is simply the container for the public key. The CA must also make the private key available via the prescribed process.

Revocation Process

One of the main benefits of a PKI system is the facility to immediately remove the ability of a fraudster to make use of a stolen card or USB device. As soon as the security of a private key is suspect—for example, if the system on which the key resides is compromised or the smartcard on which the key is stored is lost or stolen—the certificate should be revoked. This action will stop a fraudster's use of a certificate holder's identity. Note: It is necessary for relying parties to ensure their systems make use of the PKI to verify a certificate's authenticity.

There are two main options, both standards-based, for publishing revocation status.

Certificate Revocation List

The usual mechanism for the revocation of certificates is the *certificate revocation list (CRL)*. The CRL process relies on the distribution of a file containing the certificate identifiers of all revoked certificates. The file is periodically updated and can be distributed to local servers via a scheduled file transfer mechanism. Large CRLs can be segmented to reduce the network overhead associated with refreshing a CRL file, and delta updates can be supported using a mechanism that tracks each update's sequence number and periodically refreshes the full file.

Before relying on a certificate, parties should check the list of revoked certificates; if they rely on the certificate of a person whose certificate is on the CRL, the CA has no liability.

Note that the CRL operates on a negative, or exception, basis—if a certificate is *not* on the CRL, it can be trusted.

OCSP Responder

The second option for publishing certificate revocation status is the OCSP responder operation. With this approach, the CA publishes the certificate status using the Online Certificate Status Protocol format on an OCSP responder. Relying parties can do a positive check on the OCSP responder to verify a certificate's status. The protocol can be extended to enable application-specific status information (e.g., cardholder credit limit) to be associated with a certificate. OCSP is useful in large PKIs (more than 10,000 entries) because the server size remains quite static (in contrast to CRLs, which continually grow in size). The protocol supports the use of OCSP responders in a distributed environment.

One issue with OCSP responders is the overhead associated with the protocol. Responses are digitally signed, and the overhead of verifying digital signatures can adversely affect throughput. In a distributed environment, the PKI scheme must maintain local OCSP responders that are periodically updated.

Unless there is a specific reason not to, PKIs should use CRLs because they are simpler to use, require less overhead, and satisfy most revocation requirements. If additional transaction-related requirements can justify the use of OCSP responders, organizations should consider this option.

Certificate Policy and Certificate Practice Statements

All PKI schemes require two documents that users of the PKI scheme will use to ascertain the scheme's fitness for the users' purpose. The CA publishes the *certificate policy document*, which states the types and permitted uses of certificates (e.g., digital signature, encryption, special application), as well as the "chain of trust" to the root CA. The policy document also states how certificates will be signed, lists the cryptographic algorithms used to secure the keys, and provides details about the X.509 certificate fields and the validity period for certificates. The document should also identify the level of liability the CA will incur should a failure in the integrity of a certificate occur. For instance, if a certificate is revoked but does not appear in the CRL, the CA is liable if a relying party subsequently provides a product or service based on the certificate's validity.

The *certificate practice statement* is more of an operational document and indicates how the certificate policy will be enabled. The CPS typically references numerous considerations, such as who can operate as a registration authority, what level of evidence is required for the identification process used to validate participants, and how the revocation process works.

Although legal involvement is generally required, we recommend a minimalist approach to avoid the cost and inconvenience of large certificate policy and certificate practice statement documents. Note that any failure of a PKI will most likely be a failure of involved parties to adequately adhere to process, not a failure of the CA or PKI technology.

X.509 Certificate Usage

Although PKI is a mature technology based on standards, there is wide flexibility in how organizations define their certificates and how their various applications will use them. The X.509 standard defines the fields that can be included in a certificate but leaves the scheme operator significant latitude as how to populate them. (Appendix F provides more details about the X.509 specification.)

Keep in mind that the essence of a PKI system is the ability to locate a person's public key certificate (contained in the digital certificate) to verify the digital signature of the person or encrypt a message to that person. A user's certificate is typically stored on a certificate server for this purpose and will usually be retrieved by a match on the "subject" field in the certificate. This field ideally contains the certificate holder's name in an X.500 format, but this value frequently is not unique, and many operators don't use X.500 naming conventions. A common practice is to use the certificate holder's common name and append some identifier to it to make the name unique. With this

> The Electronic Health Signature Authority in Australia uses doctors' names with their provider numbers appended to it to make each entry unique. Although this approach works for the Health Insurance Commission, which uses the certificate heavily, it is less useful to external entities that do not know this number and are specifically prohibited by law from using it for other purposes.

approach, unless the relying entity knows the specific identifier for a person, it will not be able to retrieve the certificate.

One solution that some organizations employ permits the subject field to be non-unique and uses the AltSubjectName field to hold the certificate holder's email address, which normally is unique. Searches are then performed on the AltSubjectName field. This approach suits a PKI scheme that is used to sign and encrypt emails but is less satisfactory for a general-purpose PKI scheme in which users may not know the email address of the person for whom they want to find a certificate. (Note that this issue does not affect the CRL process, which uses the certificate serial number to ensure a certificate has not been revoked.)

CA Hierarchy

A CA can offer certificates for different purposes under a single authority. For instance, a CA might have a high-strength certificate protected via a robust issuance process for which operators pay a high price. For other operators who don't need such a strong certificate and would prefer not to incur a high certificate cost, the CA might issue less strong certificates under a more relaxed process and with reduced liability.

In some cases, a CA will be established with a "root" in a CA that is part of the Windows authentication framework. The CA that issues a user's certificate is important in that when the user tries to use the certificate, the system the user is accessing will use the CA's certificate to verify the authenticity of the user's certificate. If the CA's certificate is not in the user's trusted certificate repository, the system will try to access the certificate and verify its authenticity. Users will be prompted for approval to trust certificates that don't have a trusted root in the system's certificate store. Some commercial entities (e.g., Thawte, VeriSign) are, by default, in current Windows system's certificate store. For other CA certificates, users will need to explicitly load them into their system's trusted certificate store to avoid Windows security messages.

The CA hierarchy can be depicted as shown in Figure 10.5.

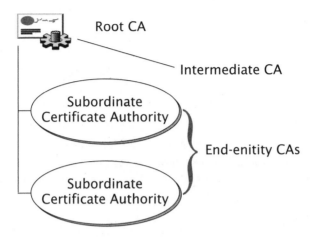

Figure 10.5: CA hierarchy

Certificate Server

The certificate server is an electronic directory, accessible by participants in the PKI community via a network that provides access for persons or systems requiring access to the public key certificate for an entity. Public certificates are typically accessed via a Lightweight Directory Access Protocol (LDAP) call based on the subjectName field in the X.509 certificate. The certificate server is typically accessed by relying parties to retrieve a certificate and get a person's public key to

- Verify the person's digital signature

- Encrypt a message to the person

All public key certificates should be placed in the certificate server directory, accessible to relying parties. In some PKI implementations, such as those in which certificates are distributed on hardware tokens that contain both the private and public key certificates, there could be pressure against deploying a certificate server. However, a certificate store should still be provided even if it is just for PKI administration purposes.

Key Generation

As noted above, the main activity of the CA is to generate key pairs for each validated participant in the PKI system. The key pair consists of a private key that is stored on some media (e.g., a smartcard) and a public key that is held in a certificate and typically stored on a certificate server.

The actual process of generating keys and distributing them varies widely and is subject to system constraints. For high-authentication systems, key generation usually occurs on token storage devices, such as smartcards. This means that a "processor" smartcard is required, and a card operating system must be selected. For less stringent security, you can generate the key pair on a secure system and store the private key on a passive token device, such as a "memory" smartcard or USB stick. An even less secure application is to email the private key to the user's system, where it is stored on the hard drive.

Certificate Management

How certificates are managed is critical to a PKI installation. Statistics indicate that approximately 20 percent of a PKI community will require the restoration of their keys on an annual basis. This requirement might be the result of lost or damaged cards or due to some compromise of the keys. In addition, because all certificates have an expiry date, a percentage of keys automatically expire each year (high-security PKIs typically allow a maximum of three years for key life, meaning 33 percent of the PKI population will be refreshed each year).

When a certificate is to be reissued, the CA generates new keys. This means that the smartcard must be redistributed to the user, and a new certificate must be placed on the server. If the certificate has been compromised or the smartcard storage device stolen, the old certificate must be placed on the revocation list. If the old key has been used to digitally sign documents, a mechanism to retain previous public keys so that signatures can still be verified may also be required.

Certificate Issues

In deciding what certificate to use, organizations must consider multiple issues:

- *To what use will the certificate be put?*—Is only a signing certificate required, or will the certificate support other uses that potentially require encryption? The certificate must state the permitted use. Most certificates are for signing only, because they are used only to authenticate users. If the certificate will be used for encryption, a mechanism to access the documents once the certificate has expired must be supported.

- *What revocation process is to be supported?*—Is a standard CRL operation satisfactory, or is an OCSP operation required? A certificate revocation list is the simpler approach, but the CRL must be maintained, and it will keep growing and needs to be accessible to all relying parties.

- *In the event of the loss or compromise of a token storage device, should the certificate be revoked?*—Although certificate revocation represents an added expense, it is more secure than storing certificate details to enable certificates to be reissued.

- *What identifier should be used in the subject field of the certificate?*— This decision is particularly important for systems that support more than one certificate scheme (i.e., if the certificates of one scheme are "cross-certified," or trusted, by another scheme).

Implementation Considerations

Let's turn our attention now to some of the implementation details and options involved with PKI.

Certificate Production

Public key certificates, also known as "digital certificates" or simply "certificates," are produced by a CA. In a certificate request, the certificate holder's credentials, including details such as cardholder PIN and a public key, are passed to the CA. The CA software formats the certificate holder's details in a prescribed format (X.509) and digitally signs the certificate with the CA's private key.

Table 10.2 summarizes the two basic options for the production of certificates: in-house and third-party. Note that a certificate must be issued at the time of the EoI check; otherwise, the reliance that can be placed on the certificate is reduced significantly.

Table 10.2: Certificate production options	
In-house certificate production	**Third-party certificate production**
Organizations issue their own certificates.	An external CA generates and signs the certificates.
Pros • Less expensive; no "cost" associated with each certificate. • Authentication level quite satisfactory for most purposes. • Simpler certificate production process.	**Pros** • Typically has a higher authentication level. • Uses the CA's registration authority process, avoiding the cost of establishment.
Cons • Certificates might not have an adequate authentication level for some applications. • Standard browsers will not recognize the certificate until it is added to the certificate store.	**Cons** • Certificate generation can impact the production of token storage devices. • Third-party certificate authorities typically charge per certificate issued.

Certificate Key Generation

This section addresses the asynchronous key pairs used in the PKI, not session keys for hardware token devices such as smartcards. Certificate keys are used for digital signing and encryption activities; card keys are used to control access to card facilities. In some cases, certificate keys may be used to establish a secure communications path to the smartcard, but typically a secure session is established using the smartcard's keys.

Possession of an applicant's public key is required for certificate production. If a smartcard is being used for token storage, the CA can produce the key pair and send the private key to the smartcard management system at the time of card production, or the card production process can have a key generation step (i.e., the keys are produced on the card, the public key is sent to the CA, and a certificate is returned).

Table 10.3 summarizes the two key generation methods.

Table 10.3: Certificate key generation options	
Off-card key generation	**On-card key generation**
Keys are generated via a hardware security module (HSM) in the card production facility or at the CA.	Keys are generated on the smartcard.
Pros • Higher throughput because dedicated hardware is used to produce the key pairs (a compute-intensive activity).	**Pros** • Highly secure because the private key never leaves the card.
Cons • Considered less secure; the private key must be protected to avoid access by a third party.	**Cons** • Certificate production is integrally tied to the smartcard production process.

If off-card key generation is used, a hardware security module is necessary. The HSM is a hardware device that is dedicated to the production and storage of cryptographic key pairs and can perform cryptographic functions. HSMs are generally designed to be tamper-proof; any attempt to physically compromise an HSM will render it useless. HSMs are "initialized" via a "key ceremony" at which trusted individuals load the device with the master key for the issuing entity (remember, the CA must digitally sign each certificate that it issues).

Refer to Appendix F regarding recommended key lengths and hashing algorithms.

Certificate Revocation

Table 10.4 summarizes the two options for certificate revocation publishing.

Table 10.4: Certificate revocation options	
Certificate revocation list (CRL)	**Online Certificate Status Protocol (OCSP)**
Revoked certificates are placed in a file that contains the certificate identifiers of all revoked certificates.	Certificate status is published in the OCSP format on an OCSP responder.
Pros • Higher throughput because the CRL protocol is simpler and entails less overhead.	**Pros** • Static in size relative to the number of issued cards.
Cons • CRLs, by definition, keep growing for the duration of the scheme.	**Cons** • OCSP lookups are digitally signed and require more processing.

Most organizations use the CRL option for the following reasons:

- There is no need for the active status of a certificate to be published.

- The potential for the CRL to grow to an unmanageable size is remote, even for large public schemes; once a certificate's validity period has expired, the certificate no longer needs to be retained in the CRL.

- CRL operations are significantly less expensive than OCSP operations.

Token Storage

A major concern for any PKI installation is the distribution of private keys because these keys must be provided to the certificate holders via a secure process. If someone were to intercept a private key, that person would be able to purport to be the certificate holder, and the certificate would need to be revoked. Distribution options include

- Encrypted electronic transmission, with the passphrase that enables the key sent via another process (e.g., hardcopy mail, secure fax)

- Managed transport via a secure storage device (e.g., smartcard, USB drive)

Organizations typically choose the first option for use in public schemes and company-wide PKIs. The second option is more appropriate for key distribution when a hardware storage device is needed for other reasons (e.g., driver license, student card). Table 10.5 summarizes the two most common hardware distribution options: smartcards and USB tokens.

Table 10.5: Key storage device options	
Smartcard	**USB token**
A plastic, wallet-sized card containing a chip for the storage of data	A device that plugs into a USB port on the host machine
Pros • Highly secure device with appropriate standards in place for interoperability	**Pros** • Widely available device that plugs directly into most PCs
Cons • Requires a smartcard reader to be connected to the PC that needs to read smartcard data	**Cons** • Not as easily transported because the device doesn't fit into a wallet

Storage Device Production

Hardware storage devices (smartcards or USB devices) can be produced in real time (i.e., at the time of the data collection and EoI check), or they can be produced in a batch mode and sent to the cardholder in the mail. Table 10.6 summarizes these two alternatives.

Table 10.6: Storage device production options	
Real-time storage device production	**Batch storage device production**
Devices are produced as soon as the necessary information has been collected. The user waits for the smartcard or USB device.	Devices are produced on high-volume production equipment in a batch process. The smartcards or USB devices are mailed to the applicants.
Pros • Saves the cost of mailing the device.	**Pros** • Efficient process and higher throughput minimize costs.
Cons • Customer wait times for device production might be perceived as excessive.	**Cons** • An interim process may be required to cover users before receipt of the storage device.

A Final Comment

PKI installations provide technically bulletproof security for digital signing and encryption purposes. The issues that arise with any PKI deployment relate to business processes. A certificate-issuing process that fails to ensure a suitably robust mechanism for verifying identities and issuing keys wastes the money spent on the system.

A PKI installation requires the organization to confront policy. The organization must decide on the level of authentication required and ensure the PKI mechanisms are sufficiently robust. Equally important is ensuring that the EoI process doesn't exceed the requirement nor place excessively onerous constraints on system users.

Discussion Questions

1. In what way is PKI the preferred answer for large-scale authentication schemes?

2. PKI is often considered too costly to implement. Suggest why this might be the case and what might be done to ameliorate costs.

3. Describe the main requirement for a certificate server and how a PKI scheme operator can obviate the need for one.

4. Why are on-card key generation schemes preferred for high-strength certificate issuance schemes?

Case Study

Refer to the case study in Appendix A in answering the following questions.

1. Would you recommend a PKI for the university?

2. What applications could be combined if the university adopted a smartcard-based certificate issuance process?

3. Would you use the same certificates for staff and students? Why or why not?

4. Many universities are adopting a federated authentication mechanism to permit research personnel from one university to access documents from other universities, with each university trusting the other's identification management system. Is PKI appropriate for this purpose? Would this environment require a high-strength or a low-strength certificate?

11

Electronic Identity Smartcards

Smartcards are the de facto standard for identity cards today for two main reasons. They are small and convenient enough to be carried in a wallet, and standards are in place that define how to use smartcards for identification purposes. These factors make smartcards more useful than USB tokens, the main competitor for smartcards in the certificate storage area. The down side to smartcards is that you must have a smartcard reader attached to your computer to read the card, whereas USB interfaces are ubiquitous.

History

Smartcards were first used in the early 1980s, but it was not until the early 1990s that they were deployed in large numbers. The number of smartcards in circulation grew exponentially during that decade, and smartcards are now in widespread use in credit card, ticketing, and mobile telephone applications. However, they have yet to be deployed in large numbers in identification applications.

The lack of standards has posed one hindrance to the deployment of smartcards in electronic identity (eID) applications. Without standards, interoperability between card schemes is severely hampered, limiting the benefit an ID card scheme operator can realize.

The situation is changing, however, and standards development is progressing well. We are now seeing the publication of guidance on deploying eID smartcards that are interoperable with other card schemes.

This development bodes well for the expanded use of smartcards in the identification sector.

A prerequisite for the widespread adoption of smartcard technology is the development and publication of standards. Let's explore this point by taking a look at the areas in which smartcards are most widely used today.

Financial Sector

The early development of standards for the use of cards in financial transactions has made the smartcard the technology of choice in the financial sector. The Europay, Mastercard, Visa (EMV) standards, which determine how a card will be used in a financial transaction and how the electronic funds transfer point of sale (EFTPOS) terminals will work with magnetic stripe and smartcards, have made it easy for the industry to use the technology worldwide. A credit card issued in the United States can be used to make transactions in Rome, with the cardholder paying the bill a month later in the United States. An Australian EFTPOS card can be tendered in London to dispense cash in the local currency.

Mobile Phone Sector

In the mobile telephone sector, one element that differentiates the Global System for Mobile Communications (GSM) market from the Code Division Multiple Access (CDMA) market is the use of Subscriber Identity Module (SIM) cards. The GSM memorandum of understanding defines how a SIM card should behave. This standardization means that a U.K. cell phone will work in Malaysia, and a call made there will appear a month later on the user's regular phone bill. The telephone industry has anticipated customer needs and has largely filled their expectations.

Ticketing Sector

Standards have developed much more slowly in the transportation ticketing sector. Vendors of ticketing systems have little incentive to promote interoperability between schemes, preferring to keep their systems proprietary. Customers have failed to force vendors to adopt open architectures because project expediencies, rather than the desire to develop the best solution for scheme operators or the traveling public, have driven most system deployments.

With the advent of "touch and go" technology, card operators are enabling banks to take a share of this market. This means that a ticketing application on a bankcard is entirely possible, frustrated only by the current proprietary nature of the ticketing schemes. The banks, realizing that many ticketing schemes carry large financial floats as customers "top up" their cards so they can travel, are likely to influence the expansion of standards development in this sector.

Identification Sector

In the electronic identification space, however, interoperability is not so advanced. The card basics (size, composition, electrical interface, and so on) have been defined in the ISO 7816 standard for many years. The Global Platform alliance has done much to promote the use of the multi-application Java Card, now the de facto standard deployment platform for smartcards, but only recently has the card architecture been embodied in an international standard, ISO 24727, enabling interoperability between card schemes to develop.

Interoperability

Interoperability greatly increases the use of an eID card and significantly reduces the inconvenience users will experience with the cards they employ. Banks have realized this benefit by combining credit card facilities, bankcard features, and ATM access on a single card. Much work has been invested in back-end integration to allow associated banks to accept each other's cards. This advance means the cardholder needs to carry only one card and remember only one PIN for banking needs.

An eID card requires the same interoperability. A single card should let the cardholder gain access to a building, provide identity at the company's HR office, and grant access to computer facilities.

The ability for an eID card scheme to interoperate with another scheme is a substantial benefit that frequently will justify the scheme itself. Without interoperability, the economic justification for the scheme is often questionable; with interoperability, the organization can spread card scheme costs over multiple applications, and cardholders realize benefits beyond the core application provided by the scheme operator.

Just as standardization in the financial sector means a credit card can be used for EFTPOS transactions, so too standardization provides benefits for eID cards. Multiple applications on the same card heighten the card's usefulness, making it more likely that the cardholder will carry it. Card scheme operators will then benefit from the potential spread of card costs over multiple applications.

Privacy

A related challenge is that of privacy. Privacy is the one issue that has the potential to derail a smartcard project. An attempt to introduce a smartcard in Ontario, Canada, was terminated in 2001 because of privacy issues. The agencies involved could not agree on a mechanism to adequately protect the privacy of their constituents. The inability to satisfactorily address privacy issues resulted in the initiative being shelved after a sunk cost of $12 million.

Privacy considerations include the following:

- What cardholder information can be collected and retained?
- How will cardholder information be kept secure?
- How will cardholder information be kept current?
- How will a cardholder be able to verify his or her information?

Card scheme operators fail to address these issues at their peril.

Fortunately, the technology is quite capable of satisfying the most stringent of privacy requirements and can accommodate multiple levels of access to card information.

At the top level, smart cards have a delegated security model that allows the card to carry multiple security domains with complete separation between the domains. This means that different applications on the card can be managed independently by separate organizations. These separate card applications can also benefit from global features such as the card security status. Once cardholders enter their global PIN and have successfully authenticated themselves to the card, applications can use this "card verified" status or request another PIN for their own specific requirement.

Most multi-application cards adopt access controls as defined under the Global Platform program. What this means is that card scheme operators can issue an eID card for cardholder identification and sell space on the card for other applications. This model not only makes card schemes more financially viable but also permits related applications to co-reside on the same card.

Deployment Issues

The decisions that eID card scheme operators must make are legion. Let's review the most common deployment issues to be faced.

Card Production System Configuration

All smartcard production systems require the following components:

- Registration system

- Smartcard management system (SCMS)

- Hardware security module (HSM)

- Collator

- Printer

Registration System

The registration authority operates the registration system, whose role is to collect the data for a user's smartcard at the time the evidence of identity (EoI) is undertaken. If the smartcard is to carry a digital certificate, the certificate must be issued as close to the EoI process as possible. Most certificate authorities will not allow issuance of a digital certificate to someone whose identity was verified some time ago.

The registration system is often a component of a business process within an organization, such as the new staff induction process.

Smartcard Management System

The smartcard management system sits between the registration system and the collator. It ensures that the data for each card is received from the registration system, and it produces a data file to be sent to the collator for card production. The data includes the information to be written to the chip—name, address, expiry date, and so on—and the data required to print the card, such as name, picture, and expiry date. If a digital certificate is to be written to the card, the SCMS interfaces to the certificate authority and the hardware security module for the generation and storage of keys.

The SCMS also manages the card information, ensuring that cards are identified with their serial numbers and date of generation recorded in a database.

Hardware Security Module

The hardware security module is a tamper-proof system used to generate and store keys. The system uses two types of keys: card keys and certificate keys. Card keys are used to secure the communications to the card. The card manufacturer provides an initial set of keys to allow the card to be written to. These keys will be changed during the personalization process when the card's security domains are created. Each security domain will have a key set.

Certificate keys are used by the certificate authority (CA) software. A public-private key pair is generated, and the public key is incorporated into the certificate. If the organization uses an external CA, the CA performs this activity; if an internal CA is used, the HSM generates the keys.

Note that if the certificate is being used for encryption purposes, the HSM might also be used to store the private keys of users.

Collator

Once the SCMS has collected all the requisite data, the data is sent to the collator. For each card, the collator prepares the data to be sent to the printer. The data to be printed on the face is sent to the print head; the data to be written to the chip is sent to the contact interface with the appropriate keys.

Printer

The printer prints the card (on one or two sides). If it uses a laser process, no other step is required. If it uses a die process, a transparent plastic film is often placed on top of the printed surface; the card is then put under the electrical contacts, and the data is written to the chip.

Figure 11.1 depicts the major components of a smartcard printing system.

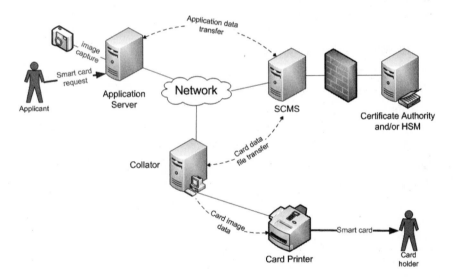

Figure 11.1: Smartcard printing system

Physical Layout

Designing the physical layout of a card is not a trivial activity. The first decision is how many faces will be printed. Cards can be either one-sided or two-sided, and although card printers are well capable of two-sided printing, this process is more expensive than single-face printing, in terms of both the extra printer time and the extra consumables that are required.

It is generally preferable to have the card manufacturer undertake as much of the printing as possible to reduce the amount required by the printer. Receiving card blanks with all the required artwork in place reduces card printing cost significantly and allows the incorporation of security features, such as micro-printing or Guilloche patterns, into the card design.

The organization will need to order card blanks in sufficient quantity to be economical for the card manufacturer. A reasonable compromise for low-volume printing is to receive the cards with a preprinted rear face (in one color) and print the front face at the time of personalization.

Data Structure

These days, virtually all smartcards are multi-application Java Cards. Part 4 of the ISO 7816 standard defines the underlying mechanisms for communicating with these cards, but as ISO 24727 is more fully adopted, card scheme operators increasingly will need to concern themselves only with the application level. This evolution is of great benefit to card application developers because of the library of application components that will be made available as the standard matures.

Most cards include an identity applet on them. Some cards have a public key infrastructure (PKI) applet for storing the cardholder's private key; the public key digital certificate is typically included as well. Applications such as these can be anticipated.

Other applications are scheme-specific and will be developed by the issuing authority. If it is a driver's licensing authority, an applet to contain driver details will be required. If the card will be used for facial recognition, a facial template will need to be stored. The card may also carry an e-purse application for small financial transactions. Each of these applications will typically have their own security domain and operate completely independently of each other.

Card Type

There are two basic types of smartcards: contact cards and wireless cards. Contact cards are simpler, while wireless cards require a small coil antenna to be placed in the plastic surrounding the chip.

As the name implies, contact cards communicate via the electrical contacts on the card face. Contact card readers must be placed wherever a need exists to read, or write to, the card. Wireless cards also need a reader, but the user simply holds the card close to the wireless reader; some auditory signal usually accompanies a read or write operation to indicate that the transaction is complete.

Contact cards are typically used when the cards store information that must periodically be read from or written to the card. Wireless cards are used for short transactions, such as e-purse applications. As a rule of thumb, any transaction that takes longer than 300 ms or must transfer more than about 1.5 kilobytes of data should use a contact card.

Cards possessing both interfaces are also available. In some cases such cards are dual-interface cards with two separate chips, or they can be hybrid cards in which both interfaces are connected to the same chip.

Card Lifecycle

Cards go through a defined lifecycle that follows a specific pattern:

1. *Manufacture*—The chip is placed into the plastic card and is initialized. Base data is written to the card at this point in the card mask. For large population card schemes, programs that are not going to change should be written at the time of manufacture because it is less expensive to put programs into the card read-only memory and saves time at the card personalization stage.

2. *Personalization*—The card scheme operator loads the applications onto the card and transfers the cardholder data. This step is performed in concert with the smartcard management system, which coordi-

nates the personalization activity and records the detail of each card printed.

3. *Issuance*—The card is provided to the cardholder. If the card is mailed to the recipient, the cardholder may be required to complete a process (e.g., PIN update) to activate the card.

4. *Locking*—The card operation may be suspended due to loss or user action. In this event, the cardholder must apply for the card to be unlocked and will usually need to present the card at a card terminal for this to occur.

5. *Termination*—The card is terminated, either due to expiration or cancellation as a result of loss or compromise. This action renders the card useless regardless of whether the card is returned or not. Terminated cards cannot be reused.

An Ideal Platform

Smartcards are the ideal platform for electronic identity cards. They are small enough to fit into a wallet and powerful enough to accommodate very strong authentication requirements. The multi-application capability of smartcards makes them the device of choice for organizations that have multiple identity-based applications, such as building access, identity card, system log-on, library, and printing service.

The choice of card type, whether contact, wireless, or a combination, will be determined by the applications being hosted on the card.

Discussion Questions

1. Give three reasons why smartcards are ideally suited for electronic identification.

2. If your identity card system did not require a PKI (i.e., no digital certificate), would you still use a smartcard or just a plastic card? Give the reasons for your choice.

3. What would be the decision criteria in selecting a local printing of cards at the time of application versus batch printing of cards, whereby cards are provided to the cardholder sometime later via mail or other distribution method?

Case Study

Refer to the case study in Appendix A in answering the following questions.

1. Would you recommend that the university issue smartcards? Give the reasons for your recommendation.

2. What applications could be combined on a smartcard if the university decided to issue such a card?

3. If the university decided to issue a smartcard, should it invite commercial entities to also use the card? Why or why not?

Appendix  A

Case Scenario

This case, provided for illustrative purposes, is based on a real identity management exercise at an Australian university. This appendix explains the identity management configuration currently in place at the university, illustrates the desired configuration, and provides a program of work to move between the two.

The solution to the case is developed progressively through the case study activities at the end of each chapter. Before completing these exercises, students should be familiar with the background detail and constraints described here.

Background

The university is distributed, with six campuses, and diverse, with three faculties each comprising multiple schools. The university accommodates more than 35,000 students, including 5,000 international students, as well as 7,000 staff and faculty members.

The "As-Is" Situation

The university's identity management environment has developed over a number of years and currently supports the main identity management requirements. Figure A.1 (at the end of this appendix) shows the current, or "As-Is," configuration.

Entry of the university's identity data is presently fragmented and laborious. The student provisioning varies widely among normal student enrollments; scholarship admissions; admissions for on-site, international, and off-shore students; and enrollment for students such as research assistants who also receive a salary. A more consistent approach would be beneficial.

Staffing starts also vary widely depending on the payroll status of the applicant. A more holistic approach and a more fine-grained categorization of staff would assist.

The Community database requires expansion to enable it to accommodate a greater range of identity management needs. It should be the authoritative source for identity management information to personnel and systems in the university.

A more robust synchronization mechanism between the main data capture systems and the Community database is required.

Library system processes are complex, and a reengineering activity to design an improved process would be beneficial.

The "To-Be" Requirement

Figure A.2 shows the desired, or "To-Be," identity management configuration.

The university requires an identity management and access control environment that improves the provisioning activity, removes redundant steps, and establishes a single authentication environment for staff and students who want to access the university's computer-based services and collaboration sites.

The identity management environment should accomplish the following goals:

- Provide for single entry of provisioning data (i.e., enter once and propagate)

- Provide a single point for de-provisioning data when a staff member leaves or is redeployed

- Maintain currency across all data repositories

- Ensure the identity management tools used in the organization support the required workflow processes

- Extend the current enterprise directory architecture to facilitate physical building access for suppliers and contractors

- Provide a common policy for password management

- Provide a harmonized unique identifier for staff and students

- Provide for appropriate compliance reporting

Constraints

It is important to recognize the current identity management environment as the starting point. The university is not a "greenfield" site—existing infrastructure and entrenched processes must accommodated. The following are considered constraints on the development of the To-Be configuration.

Zero changes to existing applications initially. To the degree possible, the deployment of identity management components should not disrupt university operational systems (Student, Staff, and Library systems). This principle recognizes that constraints exist on many of the systems currently in place in the university, and it acknowledges that the identity management program cannot unilaterally alter the access to, or provisioning from, these applications. Changes to the identity management environment will have to be made over time and staged to minimize disruption to staff and students.

Minimal change to existing processes initially. As the identity management functionality is released, there will be changes to the business processes currently used to provision identity information. Initially, however, the current provisioning processes should be maintained to avoid user resistance to too many changes at once.

"Best-of-breed" approach to vendor selection. One of the strategic decisions the university must make is whether to follow a "best-of-breed" approach, whereby the product selected for each component of the identity management program is chosen on the basis of its ability to best perform the desired function, or to follow a "product suite" approach, in which all identity management components are sourced from the same supplier. When choosing the best product for each requirement, consideration should be made of legacy systems and support for existing applications.

System Descriptions

The following paragraphs discuss the major components of the identity management environment and current issues.

Student System

The Student system is the main student record system and is populated at the time of admission and enrollment. It is used to manage a student's record for the complete student lifecycle from admission to graduation. Provisioning of the Student system is a complex process involving external regulatory and funding agencies; it is coordinated by the university's Office of the Academic Registrar.

The Student system is the authoritative data source for a student's name, address, course details, and student ID.

Issues:

- Data entry into the Student system is complex and depends on external admissions processes as well as personnel in the Office of the Academic Registrar.

- The Student system is data-intensive and is particularly vulnerable in the January–February time frame, when admissions are at a peak level.

- The library does not use the student ID number from the Student system; instead, it maintains its own numbering system.

Staff System

The Staff system is the university's human resources information service and payroll system. It maintains staff, position, and salary details and creates the payroll file.

Issues:

- Staff detail is not entered into the system in a timely way. Often, it is not until a staff member's first payroll run that the staff member's details are completely entered into the system. This means "zero-day start" is currently not possible.

- Only payrolled staff are entered into the Staff system at present. Other staff (e.g., research personnel supported by grants) are not in the system. Non-payroll staff and persons requiring "staff-like" access to university systems are entered via the Associates system to give them access to university computing resources.

- Some staff who require early or day-of-hire access to systems also receive an ID via the Associates system and subsequently have two accounts when they are finally processed through the Staff system.

- No integration exists between the Staff database and the Staff system, so detail such as current telephone number is often incorrect in the Staff system.

- No self-service exists to facilitate staff updating their details in the Staff system.

Associates System

The university uses the Associates system to provision accounts for non-staff and non-student persons. Four major groups are maintained in the system:

- Non-payroll staff
- Associates or consultants
- High-school teachers
- Professional development trainees

The system permits persons not provisioned by either the Student or the Staff system to be granted access to the university's computing resources.

Issues:

- The Associates system maintains a complete database of staff, students, and associate staff/students, but it is not considered an authoritative source for people information.

- The Associates system is viewed as a provisioning tool for persons not covered by the Staff or Students system. It is also sometimes used as a way to expedite access to university resources because accounts can be implemented more quickly via the Associates system.

Library System

The Library Services department maintains the Library system. This system manages the borrowing of the library's assets. All students and staff are issued an ID number in the system; this number is coded in a bar code on the student or staff ID card.

Issues:

- The library staff uses the Library system to manage borrowing by both students and staff. It is integrated with the Student system but assigns another ID rather than use the student ID for borrowing purposes.

- The Staff system is not integrated with the Library system, so staff details must be entered manually.

ID Card System

The ID Card system is administered by Student Services. It is used to generate both student and staff cards that identify the cardholder's role in the university. The ID Card system is integrated with the Student system so that student detail is available in the system. Staff detail must be entered manually.

The ID Card system also holds the library bar code used by the Library system. The magnetic stripe on the rear of the card allows use of the

Monitor system, an e-purse application used to pay for printing and copying.

Issues:

- No integration exists between the ID Card system and the Staff system; detail must therefore be rekeyed into the ID Card system.

Data Repositories

The university's current configuration comprises three data repositories.

Staff Directory

The main repository of contact detail within the university is the Staff database, a standalone application maintained by IT Services. The system stores

- Common name
- Location
- Position
- Telephone number
- Email address
- Picture (JPEG format)

An online facility, accessible from the university portal, provides an electronic form and approval workflow to update the Staff database, but data entry is manual.

Issues:

- The Staff database is not integrated with the Staff system identity data repository or the Associates system for non-payroll staff. For this reason, double entry of staff detail is occurring, and a high probability of error between data repositories exists.

- While the Staff database is highly visible and therefore typically up-to-date, there is no requirement to ensure that a staff member's proper name is used or spelled correctly.

- In some cases, a staff member with two roles on campus may have two entries in the Staff database.

Active Directory

Active Directory (AD) provides directory services for Windows environments at the university. It provides authentication for both staff and students as well as access control for some applications, such as the Microsoft Exchange email system.

AD has the potential to support group management and policy enforcement, but the university has not exploited these capabilities.

Issues:

- Group management is not widely employed. The university maintains five main groups: staff, staff-like, student, student-like, and associate. No differentiation exists between academic and administrative staff, nor is there any segmentation by faculty or college.

- While establishment of accounts from the Student, Staff, and Associates systems is automated, group assignments and shared folders access are administered manually.

- There is no leveraging of AD groups for access control decisions.

- No definition of authoritative data sources is currently maintained.

Community Database

The Community database is an Oracle database consisting of the following tables:

- Member ID—Provides a cross-reference table
- Identity—Contains the main identity information
- Staff Contact—Contains contact detail
- Occupancy—Contains position detail

This database is the authoritative source for identity information for approximately 30 applications. It contains more than 150,000 records.

The Community database is controlled by the IT department, which manages the update and maintenance of the data. The school uses a standard extract, transform, and load (ETL) tool to synchronize data from applications to the Community database.

Issues:

- The Community database was established as part of a pilot project that was put into production. Its schema and structure do not provide the flexibility and extensibility to support future identity management developments.

Program of Work

The development of the optimal identity management environment depicted in Figure A.2 is a multistage process that will span a significant time frame. The main activities are as follows.

Activity 1: Policy Definition and Core Directory Establishment

A core component of the identity management facilities is an Enterprise Directory. Activity 1 establishes a core directory for the storage of identity data and a synchronization tool to populate it. A central identity store is required to provide improved access to identity information without adversely affecting the current authentication service provided by the Active Directory.

Activity 1 will have a largely "behind-the-scenes" impact on the university. Users should experience fewer errors. Confusion between similar identities will be reduced, and support personnel will appreciate the more comprehensive and ordered structure of the directory. Users of the new white-pages application will notice a faster response and the availability of a richer data set.

Activity 2: Identity Management and Automatic Provisioning

Activity 2 has two components: implementation of the provisioning engine to populate the Enterprise Directory and deployment of the Virtual Directory functionality for authentication.

Automating the provisioning processes will afford the first significant benefit for users. It will reduce the labor-intensive activity of data entry and will improve the accuracy of data in the Enterprise Directory. This stage will provide a provisioning system that will encompass the current provisioning that occurs in the Staff, Associates, and Staff Directory systems.

Activity 2 will primarily impact personnel currently involved in the provisioning of staff records. Student Services personnel provisioning into the ID Card system and Library staff provisioning into the Library system will also notice it. Data will appear more quickly, and there will be less data entry to perform.

Activity 3: Workflow-based Provisioning

Once automated provisioning is in place, the university can deploy the workflow functionality. This step depends completely on a business process reengineering activity, and because provisioning is far more efficient in a role-based environment, commencement of a role engineering task is a prerequisite.

At the close of Activity 3, the university will operate a largely automated and robust identity provisioning and de-provisioning process. The system will accommodate the requirements of the individual schools and specific administrative business units.

The system will significantly improve the commencement experience of both staff and students. Staff will be able to access university resources on their first day of work; no "workarounds" to obtain temporary access will be required. Student provisioning will also be improved with no appreciable delay between enrollment and system access.

Activity 3 will offer significant cost savings because minimal manual intervention will be required to establish and maintain identity records for staff and students. This activity requires no additional deployment of software but will necessitate configuration of job queues, activation of real-time listeners, and enabling of audit logs.

Activity 4: Web Single Sign-On (SSO)

The university is increasingly employing Web-based applications, making implementation of a standardized Web single sign-on (SSO) facility more important. Where these applications are deployed in an externally hosted environment, the authentication process is further complicated. It is noted that once the Web SSO infrastructure is in place, it will still be necessary to enable each Web application. Use of the Web SSO environment will grow over time as new Web applications are added.

Activity 4 will be highly visible within the university community. The provision of a single sign-on facility for Web applications will resolve a chronic issue that currently requires users to re-enter their user name and password when moving between applications. Business needs and application-specific capabilities will determine the development and deployment of Web SSO.

As users request SSO to extend to externally hosted applications, pressure to complete Activity 5 (federated authentication) is likely to increase.

Activity 5: Federated Authentication

The federated authentication facility will provide the ability for staff and students to access externally hosted applications without the need to pass authentication data to the hosting entity. As users log on to these applications, the infrastructure will securely access the university's authentication infrastructure to retrieve the appropriate access rights for each user.

The university will deploy the federated authentication infrastructure over time. As new externally hosted applications are added, the workload to provide access for remote personnel will decrease. It is recommended that a commercial federated authentication product be acquired for externally hosted production applications.

The provision of federated authentication is important to the university from two main points of view:

- The university must participate in a geographically dispersed research community. It is cost-prohibitive for each research institution to maintain access control lists to all their research facilities in order to provide global access. Federation provides the ability for one university to trust the identity management facilities of another and to grant access to remote personnel on the basis of that trust.

- The university in some cases hosts Web applications externally. This means that either a secure mechanism to externally distribute the authentication attributes for staff and students must be designed or a federated authentication model should be adopted.

To accommodate these requirements, a federated authentication infrastructure should be deployed for the university.

Activity 6: Server Account Management

As noted in the university's environmental scan document, improved system management tools for Unix and Windows systems administration are highly desirable. At the earliest point in the identity management program, Unix administration should be provided with a reporting tool that will combine the access control lists on each Unix partition to help system administrators maintain Unix accounts, including those on VMware partitions. When advisable, a tool to facilitate central administration of Unix accounts should be acquired and deployed.

The deployment of a server account management tool will dramatically affect the administration of servers within the university and will address a potential security concern. Activity 6 will provide

- Integration of Linux, MacOS, and Unix systems into the AD domain

- Improved audit and reporting ability

The steps in deploying the server account management facility are as follows:

1. *Selection of the tool to be used*—The initial activity is to define the requirements for the university and select the preferred tool. This selection should be based on a comparison of the capabilities of the indicated products against the documented requirements. A presentation on the proposed products may be warranted.

2. *Installation and configuration of the selected tool*—Once the preferred tool has been acquired, it must be configured for each server that is to be part of the managed server environment.

This activity is mutually exclusive from the other activities and can proceed at any time.

Activity 7: Role Management and Fine-grained Authorization

The adoption of fine-grained access control is a function of the applications using the Enterprise Directory for program authorization. The directory will be capable of responding to requests for policy-based attributes. Applications must have the capability to use these attributes and apply security policies appropriately.

The deployment of fine-grained authorization will give the university sophisticated access-control capabilities for those applications equipped to use it.

Exercise

Consider the activities outlined above and the required (To-Be) configuration. Sequence the tasks in a logical order that ensures prerequisites are performed before dependent tasks. In designing your roadmap, consider the following:

- What activities are likely to continue for a long time (i.e., be performed concurrently with other activities)?

- What activities can be done at any point in the program (i.e., do not depend on another activity)?

- What activities have minimal cost but promise significant return on investment? Where should these activities occur in the program?

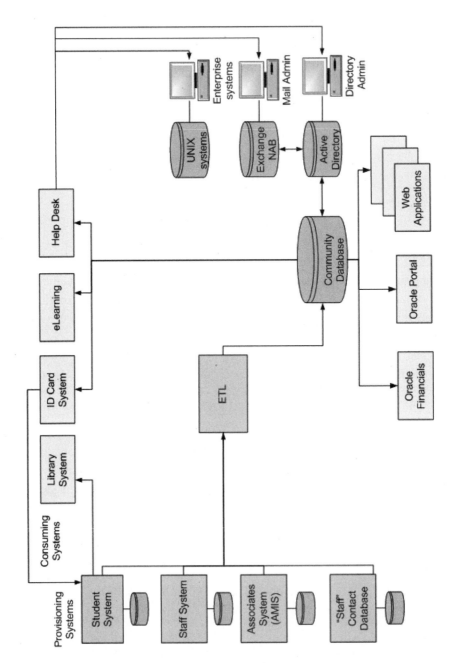

Figure A.1: "As-Is" configuration

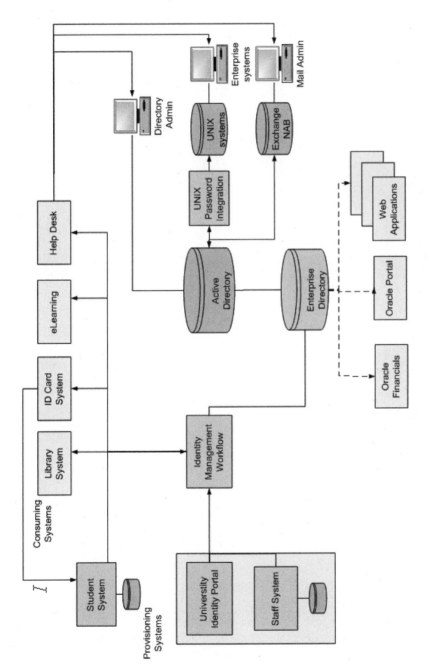

Figure A.2: "To-Be" configuration

Appendix B

Standards

One of the most important aspects of selecting and deploying an identity management environment is adherence to standards. The identity management arena is characterized by a number of niche product suppliers that are specialists in their own particular aspect of identity management (e.g., provisioning, federated authentication, single sign-on). To interoperate with other components of the identity management environment, it is important for these products to adhere to standards so that they can be interfaced to other components of the solution.

No one set of standards can completely define the identity management requirement. The area is so diverse that standards in several areas must be included. The following categories provide a good starting point to determine which standards should be considered.

Directory Standards

When selecting a directory product, it is important to ensure that it adheres to the standards appropriate for its use.

Directory infrastructure. The X.500 standard is the main standard for directories. X.500 defines the structure of a directory information tree (DIT) for a directory. It defines how entities are categorized within a worldwide naming structure with country, state, organization, organizational unit, and name attributes that can be used. Within the X.500 structure, an interoperable directory can be defined with a rich namespace that can suit any organizational structure.

X.500 also defines the Directory Access Protocol (DAP), which stipulates how entries in the directory are to be accessed. Few organizations currently use X.500 directories due to the overhead associated with designing and managing them.

All commercial X.500 directories support the Lightweight Directory Access Protocol (LDAP) as an access protocol, as well as the LDAP Data Interchange Format (LDIF) as an interface specification.

Access protocol. LDAP is not a directory standard; it simply defines the access protocol for a directory. As the name implies, LDAP represents a simplification of the DAP standard and provides for conformity (and therefore interoperability) between directories. Unfortunately, many LDAP directories are not directories at all but simply databases with an interface that can respond to an LDAP request.

Directory attributes. Standards are available for most entities one would want to store in a directory. The de facto standard for a person entity is inetOrgPerson, first defined by Netscape in the 1990s. RFC 2798 defines the schema. Microsoft has given tacit approval to this schema but has changed it slightly, calling it iNetOrgPerson (note the capital "N"). Other schema definitions to be considered are the organizationalPerson and eduPerson extensions.

Authentication Standards

Several standards are appropriate for the authentication task.

Digital certificate. The X.509 V3 standard is well accepted as the definition of a digital certificate. The certificate normally contains the public key for the entity in question. The certificate is identified by its serial number and is typically accessed via the Subject attribute or the altSubjectName attribute. RFC 2459 defines the use of these attributes, but each system defines its own specific use of them, so the level of interoperability among public key infrastructure (PKI) systems is low.

Many public key cryptography standard (PKCS) routines use a person's X.509 certificate for digital signing or encryption tasks. For instance, PKCS #11 defines how to connect to a storage device, such as a smartcard containing an X.509 certificate, to query the certificate and perform cryptographic functions. For a complete listing of these interface standards, see Appendix D.

Federated authentication. Security Assertion Markup Language (SAML) 2.0 defines how credentials (i.e., identity data for a specific entity) should be formatted so that they can be passed between components of the identity management environment. For example, if an application needs to know the access rights for a particular user requesting permissions, this information should be passed in a SAML message and parsed accordingly.

Although SAML describes the protocol for exchanging credentials, it does not define the credentials themselves. For this purpose, it is necessary for a federated authentication mechanism to define the specific implementation to be adhered to and establish agreement on the attributes to be used. Shibboleth, with the eduPerson extensions to inetOrgPerson, is one such implementation used extensively in academia.

Fine-grained access control. Extensible Access Control Markup Language (XACML) defines the standard for the use of identity credentials in access control environments. It goes beyond simple access control lists used by applications to determine who can and cannot access the application. XACML provides both a schema and a decision language to enable administrators to employ complex rules to determine access permissions in real time. Access rights can easily be modified by location of log-on, time of day, and so on.

Appendix C

Glossary

ACL—Access control list; determines the level of access a user is entitled to receive within the target application

AD—Active Directory; provides authentication directory services in Windows environments

Authentication—Granting users the right to access a computer or a network of computers

Authorization—Assignment of application access rights to users

CRL—Certificate revocation list

De-provision—To remove entitlements for an account

Directory—A software product capable of storing identity details

Disable—To make access to an account inoperable

Distinguished name—A name that uniquely identifies a record in a directory

DIT—Directory information tree

Domain—The environment in which a person or entity has an identity definition

Entitlement—Definition of access permissions in a computer application

ETL—Extract, transform, and load; typically refers to loading data into a data store

Federated authentication—An authentication environment in which there are multiple providers of identity information and multiple service providers consuming that information

HSM—A hardware device that is dedicated to the production and storage of cryptographic key pairs and can perform cryptographic functions

Identity—Defining attributes of a person or entity within a digital community

Identity management—Organizing the collection, storage, and disbursement of data specific to people in the organization and to persons and companies external to the organization

Identity store—A directory or database that contains identity detail

LDAP—Lightweight Directory Access Protocol; a standard that defines how entities in a directory can be accessed

Namespace—Defines how the objects in a directory are related, providing a hierarchy that determines how the data is stored and retrieved

OCSP—Online Certificate Status Protocol

PAM—Pluggable Authentication Module; Unix facility to facilitate centralised authentication

PAM—Privileged Account Management; control of generic accounts with elevated privileges

PKI—A mechanism to provide digital document signing and document encryption through the use of a key pair consisting of a public key and a private key

Provision—To populate the identity stores in an organization

RACF—Resource Access Control Facility; an authentication database typically used on IBM mainframes

RBAC—Role-based access control; the process of granting access to an organization's computer programs based on the role a person fulfills in the organization

Referential integrity—A feature of a directory service whereby the data of a record is always maintained accurately regardless of how many information tree branches it might be spread over

Replication—An internal directory feature by which the directory, or a portion thereof, is copied to another location

Repudiation—The denial (by a user) of the validity of a transaction

Role—An individual's distinct functional association with the digital community

SaaS—Software As a Service (externally hosted application)

SAML—Security Assertion Markup Language

Schema—Attributes stored in a directory as defined in the directory information tree

Self-service—The ability of users to make changes to their identity record

Server account—A generic account used to let one server access another controlled server

Service account—A generic account enabling user access based on the user's logged-on system (not the user's identity)

SPML—Service Provisioning Markup Language

SSO—Single sign-on; the use of one password to sign on to multiple applications

Synchronization—Automatically updating a data repository from a source repository either on a batch or an event-driven basis

Validation—The check of identity source documents as part of an enrollment process

Virtual directory—A facility that provides access to data from multiple sources, including directories and databases, and presents that data in a single view

Web SSO—The capability for Web-based applications to share the same log-in environment

XACML—Extensible Access Control Markup Language; a policy language that lets application administrators set access control parameters for users of their applications

Public Key Cryptography Standards

For full documentation of the following public key cryptography standards (PKCSs), visit the RSA Laboratories Web site at *http://www.rsa.com/rsalabs/node.asp?id=2124.*

Standard	Description
PKCS #1: RSA Cryptography Standard	Defines the key implementation details for the RSA public key algorithm.
PKCS #3: Diffie-Hellman Key Agreement Standard	Describes the Diffie-Hellman standard for the exchange of secret keys between two parties over a public network.
PKCS #5: Password-Based Cryptography Standard	Describes how to use public key cryptography to generate encryption keys for encrypted documents.
PKCS #6: Extended-Certificate Syntax Standard	Defines how to store information in attributes within a signed certificate; requires the scheme operator to define their use.
PKCS #7: Cryptographic Message Syntax Standard	Defines ASN.1 data structures for cryptographic messages.
PKCS #8: Private-Key Information Syntax Standard	Describes the ASN.1 layout for a private key.
PKCS #9: Selected Attribute Types	Provides a glossary of data structures used in the PKCS standards.

Standard	Description
PKCS #10: Certification Request Syntax Standard	Documents the ASN.1 data structures for communicating a certificate request to a certificate authority.
PKCS #11: Cryptographic Token Interface Standard	Defines hardware security token access. This large standard provides a high-level interface to the most common security token operations.
PKCS #12: Personal Information Exchange Syntax Standard	Describes the way to exchange private keys when supported. Most schemes will not allow private keys to leave the secure storage facility (smartcard or hardware storage module).
PKCS #13: Elliptic Curve Cryptography Standard	Public key infrastructure (PKI) certification bodies are increasingly mandating use of elliptic curve cipher suites for signing and hashing.
PKCS #15: Cryptographic Token Information Format Standard	Defines how PKI data should be stored within smartcard files. The standard allows PKI functions to be enabled via the standard 7816-4 common command set.

X.509 Specification

The main attributes of certificates that adhere to the X.509 standard are as follows:

- *Version*—This field identifies which version of the X.509 standard applies to the certificate, which affects the information that can be specified in the certificate. Version 3 certificates should be used.

- *Serial Number*—The certificate authority (CA) is responsible for assigning a unique serial number to each certificate. This information is used, for example, when a certificate is revoked; the certificate's serial number is placed in a certificate revocation list (CRL).

- *Signature Algorithm Identifier*—This field identifies the algorithm used by the CA to sign the certificate. It will most likely be RSA with a SHA-1 secure hash algorithm.

- *Issuer Name*—This field holds the X.500 name of the entity that signed the certificate, which is the organization operating the CA. Using the certificate implies trusting the entity that signed it.

- *Validity Period*—Each certificate is valid for only a limited amount of time. This period is described by a start date and time and an end date and time.

- *Subject Name*—This field contains the name of the certificate holder identified in the certificate. This name typically uses the

X.500 standard, so it must be unique across the Internet. A typical distinguished name (DN) of an entity might be, for example:

CN=John Citizen1234567, OU=Driver Licence, O=Queensland Transport, C=AU

- *Subject Public Key Information*—This field holds the public key of the entity being named, together with an algorithm identifier that specifies which public key cryptographic system this key belongs to and any associated key parameters.

A number of extensions, the use of which will need to be determined, are also available for the X.509 standard:

- *Key Usage*—Should typically be set for digital signing and critical

- *Extended Key Usage*—If encryption is to be supported, can be set for encipherment (must not be set critical)

- *Certificate Policies*—Should contain the object identifier (OID) of the organization

- *CRL Distribution Point*—Should indicate the URL where the CRL can be accessed

- *Subject Key Identifier and Authority Key Identifier*—Should be used to identify the trusted root

- *Subject Alternative Name*—Should contain the cardholder's email address

- *Basic Constraints*—For most user certificates, should indicate CA=null

Key Lengths

The key length for the key pair used in a public key infrastructure (PKI) scheme is important. The longer the key length, the longer it would take someone to "break" the key but also the longer it will take to perform a signing or encryption activity. The following are the recommended Public Key Certificate Algorithm key lengths for client certificate digital signatures for up to about the year 2012.

- Digital Signature Algorithm (DSA) with a modulus of 1,024 bits and SHA-1 hash

- RSA 2,048-bit key and a SHA-256 hash

- Elliptic Curve DSA (ECDSA) (Curve -P 224 bits)

For higher-security client certificates, consideration should be given to adopting a longer key length, as provided by the latter two choices above. The elliptic curve option is generally considered the preferred longer-term strategic solution.

Note that the U.S. National Institute of Standards and Technology (NIST) recommends a move from SHA-1 to SHA-2 by the end of 2010, but this step might be impractical until sufficient clients can support this standard. Those organizations with modest security requirements should consider delaying the move.

Index
